LONELINESS is for loving

AVE MARIA PRESS
Notre Dame Indiana 46556

LONELINESS
is for loving

Robert E. Lauder

**To my mother, father and sister
whose love liberated me from my loneliness**

Grateful acknowledgment is made to the *Long Island Catholic*
for permission to reprint those portions of this book which
originally appeared in its pages.

Library of Congress Catalog Card Number: 77-94033

International Standard Book Number: 0-87793-147-X (paperback)
0-87793-148-8 (cloth)

Design and typography: Cae Esworthy

Photography: Orville Andrews, 128. Patrick J. Gibbs, 44, 86.
Patrick Mooney, 32-33. Notre Dame Publications
Office, 102. Anthony Rowland, 4-5. Vernon
Sigl, 8, 12, 24, 66-67, 114-115. David Strickler,
54, 78, 136-137. Lucille Sukalo, cover.

Printed and bound in the United States of America.

Contents

Introduction

A perceptive friend who had battled loneliness and reflected long on its meaning once told me that the drive to overcome loneliness motivates people more than anything. She thought this was the strongest drive behind most human activities. She was a hair's breadth from the truth. What motivates people more than anything else is the need to be loved. Though closely related to loneliness, the drive for love is more radical, more existential, more personal.

Loneliness may be the most widespread problem in America today. Like certain physical diseases, it is no respecter of persons. In 1975, a survey taken by the Canadian Catholic Conference to pinpoint people's concerns found it to be a major problem. Summing up the report the director wrote, "From coast to coast, by young people as well as old, by rich as well as poor, loneliness is identified as a major personal and social problem." In the fall of 1976, in an attempt to find out what issues interested people in a presidential campaign year, a study done in New York State by the Department of Mental Hygiene revealed that the fundamental problem for many was being alone.

There is no special type of person who is saved
from this threat; there is no moment in life when
the battle is won once and for all. There are partial
victories; it probably will return to fight another day.

Loneliness is the feeling of not really mattering
to anyone, of not being significant, of being
isolated, of being alone in the sense of not being
important to anyone. This feeling can occur at any
time in an individual's life; it can affect the young
and the elderly, the busy and the leisurely, the
reflective and the unreflective.

Feelings of loneliness can be severe or passing.
Those whose experience is only slight should not
underestimate the problem. In an interview in which
she was discussing poverty, Mother Teresa of
Calcutta, the great servant of the poor, remarked,
"Maybe in the United States we don't see the
hungry and the naked and the homeless in the
streets. But I think there is a much greater poverty,
and that is very spiritual poverty. If you come to the
place where we are trying to spread love and
compassion [India], I think you will understand
better how poor our people are, how much more
there is hunger for understanding love. I believe it is
easier to relieve material poverty. By giving to a
person who is hungry for a piece of bread or for a
plate of rice, you have already solved the difficulty.
But, I think, the people who are hurt, who are
lonely, who are unwanted, who are hopeless, who
are those like the alcoholics and the people who
have forgotten how to smile, who have forgotten
what are human love and human touch. . . . I
think that is very great poverty."

Loneliness is one of the most disturbing effects
of spiritual poverty. It can be a symptom of our
uncaring society. It need not crush people. They
need not be defenseless victims before its assaults.
The individual can fortify himself or herself with
battle plans.

This book presents such a plan — a plan for people to understand, combat and use loneliness for personal growth. The plan is rooted in the meaning and mystery of personal existence and in the model of human existence provided by the life, death and resurrection of Jesus.

Chapter One

Loneliness and Living

Loneliness is part of the human condition, though different styles of living may either accent or relieve its presence. There is for human persons no Shangri-la from which loneliness is banished. Some people may feel more lonely than others, but those who completely deny the existence of their loneliness may be in the worst shape of all. To be ignorant of loneliness or to deny its reality is to deceive yourself and perhaps to misunderstand what human living is all about.

There may be certain periods in life when persons are more susceptible to loneliness than others. Twice a month I offer Mass at a home for the aged. The home is a good example of how such an institution should be run. Yet the faces looking into mine during the Eucharist seem to be lonely faces. Those who must spend their last days in institutions must at least from time to time have strong feelings of loneliness. They must occasionally feel that they don't count, that they don't matter, that they are not significant. When people age and the specter of death becomes more and more real, the threat of loneliness can be severe and be rivalled only by fear of death.

Youth No Exception

Besides old age, the period of life most suscepti-ble to feelings of loneliness is adolescence. The need for comradeship seems particularly strong at this time. The adolescent needs affirmation as he or she moves toward adult personhood. If that affirmation is lacking, loneliness can seem over-whelming. The sentiment expressed by the teenage girl in Carson McCuller's play, *A Member of the Wedding,* seems to be a universal experience of adolescence: "Shush, just now I realized something. The trouble with me is that for a long time I have been just an 'I' person. All other people can say 'we'. . . . All people belong to a 'we' except me."

Children also experience loneliness. The small girl who doesn't want her parents to go out in the evening dreads being lonely. She may not be able to articulate her feelings, but her tears reveal them vividly. The presence of her parents is so neces-sary for her peace that she doesn't wish them to leave her even for an evening. The little boy who when he can't sleep cries for his mother and father feels terribly alone. The presence of a parent will help him surrender to sleep and spend a peaceful night.

Both married people and single adults are sus-ceptible to feelings of loneliness. A mother who has raised her family can feel that her job has been done and that she no longer matters or counts. Having rooted her personal fulfillment in what she had been doing for her children, she feels, when there is nothing more to do for them, that her role in life, hence her life, is finished.

The unmarried person lacks one of the most obvious and powerful antidotes to loneliness — a loving mate. While married people are also subject to loneliness, every married person has the presence of another as a personal sign that he or she does matter deeply to someone. The single person has no such sign. Though friends can provide tremendous support, the reality behind the words "for better or worse until death us do part" is a unique kind of presence.

The unmarried are in an especially difficult situation in American society because of the often unarticulated but very real myth that everyone should get married. Not to be married means in American society to have failed or to be odd. The single person pays for his or her unmarried state.

By giving women a sense of their innate dignity and importance, the women's liberation movement has erased, to some extent, the stigma attached to women who are unmarried. Some women have the strength to resist society's erroneous judgment that a woman can't be fulfilled unless she is married.

Built into Celibate Life

The celibate vocation has loneliness built into it, but what makes feelings of loneliness more intense today for the priest or religious is that celibacy exists within a secular society. Within a Christian community the celibate can receive much encouragement and respect because the value of his celibacy is appreciated. In a secular society the person's celibacy is one more anachronism, one more sign of irrelevance.

Since my ordination to the priesthood in 1960 I have experienced a 180-degree turn in people's attitude toward priests. When I was first ordained, respect for the priest was at a high among both Catholics and non-Catholics. Though the latter did not share the world view of the priest, they admired what they took to be lives of dedication and service. Many Catholics treated priests with excessive respect ranging from blind agreement because "Father says so" to believing that the priest had some kind of priority on relationship with God. Thank God, the excessive respect has gone. With it among many Catholics, however, has gone appreciation of the vocation to the priesthood.

It seems that the secular society has eroded the meaning of the priesthood in the awareness of many Catholics. Frequently, even with people who personally like me, I am aware of an unstated confusion over why anyone would be a priest today. To put the confusion into some form it might be stated as, "You seem like a nice guy, fairly intelligent and talented. Why would you want to be a priest? Doesn't that seem to be wasting your life?"

The loneliness built into the celibate vocation is intensified because of the diminished respect for priestly existence. I know I have experienced loneliness, the feeling of not mattering, of not being significant, because of the views of many of my contemporaries. Every adult wants to feel that his or her life is meaningful, that he or she is making some kind of contribution to the human community. Many people experience this through their children. I believe in priestly ministry but I don't experience much support for my belief. Perhaps that very experience could be calling me to growth.

Further Reflections

Though no age of life escapes feelings of loneliness, a particular society can contribute strongly to such feelings. A consumer society fosters loneliness in a special way because of its emphasis on the importance of things. People are encouraged to judge themselves by the things they possess. We are so inundated by absurd advertising that we fail to reflect on what such advertising really is telling us. Pick any commercial on television and assume a critical distance from it. Ask yourself the following questions: What is the commercial saying about me? To what is it appealing in me? By what values is it asking me to live? It's a good bet that it is giving me a dangerously false self-image. It may be telling me that I am what I possess. A steady diet of such advertising can strongly influence both our consciousness and our conscience. We can start judging people, both others and ourselves, by their possessions . . . by their financial success, their wardrobe, or the size and price of their automobile. It's a frightening frame of mind to experience but easy to slip into. To judge the value of personal existence by the possessions accumulated is to court loneliness.

Loneliness in Art Form

Contemporary artists have brilliantly depicted the plague of loneliness that strains contemporary persons' attempts to live meaningfully. A vivid artistic image of the inevitable loneliness that surrounds a person who has based his life on the possession of things is one of the last scenes of Orson Welles' film masterpiece, *Citizen Kane*. The multimillionaire Charlie Kane (brilliantly played by Orson Welles) has spent his life collecting things. He has never been able to love anyone, and he has continually tried to buy the love of the people who knew him. At the end of the film, after Charlie Kane has died, the camera pans to view all the expensive objects he has bought during his life, hundreds of objects with which Charlie Kane tried to remove his feelings of loneliness. Through the eye of the camera we see the effects of a life centered on things, a life that ended in extreme loneliness.

A classic example of a lonely man is Arthur Miller's character, Willy Loman, in *Death of a Salesman*. All through his adult life, Willy wanted to be a success, and he saw the road to success through the superficial relationships he developed in being a salesman. Whether he is urging his son to be a popular football hero in high school or asking his next-door neighbor what the secret of success is, Willy reveals his false set of values. When he is on a sales trip, Willy, because of extreme loneliness, commits adultery. When he is caught by his son, whom he had filled with false values, Willy receives no absolution from the boy when he confesses, "She's nothing to me, Biff. I was lonely, I was terribly lonely." At the end of the play, at Willy's graveside, Biff sums up Willy's problem, "He had the wrong dreams. All, all, wrong."

Such great contemporary European film directors as Ingmar Bergman, Federico Fellini and Michelangelo Antonioni time and time again have probed contemporary persons' intense feelings of loneliness. Recently a popular American film, *Taxi Driver,* which won the Cannes award as best film of 1976, depicted the experience of a totally alienated young veteran in New York. Striving to battle his oppressive loneliness, the young taxi driver frequents porno films and watches hours and hours of television. Failing in most of the human relationships he tries, he finally makes contact through violence. For all its horror, *Taxi Driver* follows a clear line of logic: somehow every person has to make contact with someone. If the experience of loneliness can't be overcome any other way, violence will be tried.

Contemporary literature from Kafka to Bellow often focuses on the loneliness of persons. The recent best seller, *Looking for Mr. Goodbar,* by Judith Rossner, whatever its literary merits, presents an interesting example of the kind of aberrant activity to which loneliness can lead a young woman living alone in New York.

Though art may deal with the more extreme and dramatic forms of loneliness, it is only accenting and highlighting a basic experience that everyone has at some moment in life, and some have for long periods in their lives.

Personal Testimony

One of the loneliest years in my life was my first year of graduate work. It was also the toughest year I have had in my 17 years of priestly ministry. It was the least fulfilling year for me emotionally.

I was asked by my Bishop to go away to study in order to obtain a graduate degree in philosophy. The Bishop was planning to build a college seminary and he was starting to round up a faculty. The invitation seemed to come at the worst possible time in my life. My only sister had just died, leaving two infants. My mother and father, their hearts breaking, tried to bear up. As a parish priest I was stationed near my parents' home and my presence, even in a brief visit, meant a great deal to them. Now the Bishop was asking me to go to another city to study. After prayer and counsel, I chose to accept the Bishop's invitation.

As I write this, memories of that very difficult first year of graduate study vividly zoom into my memory. I was 30 years old and attending classes with many who had recently graduated from college. Though I hadn't formally studied philosophy for eight years, I found myself in the same classroom with people who had put in two, three and even more years in graduate work. I was confused by the academic material and the goal of a doctorate seemed unattainable.

I was worried about my family. As an active parish priest working with various Catholic Action groups, I had built up strong relationships with many parishioners. The people with whom I worked were always affirming me. Working with them was very fulfilling and personally rewarding.

Most of the ties seemed severed by my leaving the parish. I found myself in strange surroundings, doing study that was not at all interesting. From being someone who played an important role in the lives of many I was suddenly in a situation in which I didn't seem to matter to anyone. I was just part of a crowd.

Feeling very lonely I used to go for walks at night. Often I would recite the rosary. Prayer helped me to keep my present situation in perspective. I needed reminding that what I was involved in was important. As I was preparing to leave the parish two college-age girls with whom I had shared a great deal during my parish experience gave me a gift. With the gift one of them included a few lines from a Robert Frost poem, "Stopping by Woods on a Snowy Evening" —

> The woods are lovely, dark and deep,
> But I have promises to keep,
> And miles to go before I sleep,
> And miles to go before I sleep.

My friend was communicating to me her love and concern. She was saying that, though it would have been nice to stay in the parish with those to whom I had grown so close, I "had promises to keep" and "miles to go before I sleep." As I walked around the university grounds at night, feeling extreme loneliness, I used to repeat those lines from Frost. The lines reminded me that my feelings of insignificance, my feelings of unimportance, were not true. The lines reminded me of a mission, a journey I had undertaken.

Circumstantial Loneliness
As was indicated in the introduction, loneliness is a feeling, a feeling of not being significant, of not counting, of not mattering to anyone. There is no essential connection between feeling lonely

and being alone. A person can feel very lonely and yet be in a crowd; a person can be physically alone and yet have a strong sense of personal value. The successful businessman or salesman may be very lonely; the Trappist monk may rarely experience loneliness.

Strange circumstances can foster loneliness. A nun I know teaches at a seminary. Though she is surrounded by people most of the day she frequently feels lonely at the seminary. As a female in a male's world, she feels the need for affirmation and she finds that she doesn't always receive it. Though she is well liked, perhaps many of the males at the school are insensitive to a woman's feelings. Probably a moment's empathy would reveal to them how alone the sister must feel in a man's world.

For me feelings of loneliness sometimes occur at parties. This can happen even when I know rather well those attending the party. It's difficult to explain why the feeling of loneliness comes. I don't fully understand it. Suddenly I feel left out or not part of the group. Sometimes longtime friendships become questionable. Why should this happen at a party? It must be that the expected joyousness and camaraderie is not experienced and this allows other feelings to take over. In the midst of the celebrating I can look at close friends and wonder how deep friendships are. Strange that something as beautiful as friendship which can seem so clear and strong in moments of disappointment, suffering and tragedy can become doubtful in the midst of a party. In one of Albert Camus' writings when a character's suicide is being investigated, someone explains the deceased's action by saying that his best friend spoke to him in a disinterested tone of voice. Loneliness underlines the fragility of friendships.

At least in its extreme form, loneliness might be

described as the feeling of being existentially alone, of being in an unfriendly universe, of being a function which has only pragmatic value. A popular image of loneliness is a poor, elderly person, apparently abandoned, living in a tenement flat. An equally valid image would be a corporation president, surrounded by his employees, sitting in a plush office. The meaning of loneliness is not tied up with the number of people who physically are present to you but rather the way or manner in which you are present to others and to yourself.

Loneliness can emerge very strongly at strange times. A friend of mine reported an incident that illustrates how loneliness can be quite devastating if we aren't prepared for it. My friend, in her mid-40's, had just recently lost her father whom she had taken care of for the last 10 years of his life. A couple of months after her father's death, she was attending the wake of a friend's parent. When she entered the funeral parlor, no one whom she knew was present. She sat down to wait and noticed that there were various small groupings of people talking. She was the only person at the wake who was alone. Every other person was in some group, however small. Suddenly she felt very lonely and the thought occurred to her: "This is how it will be for the rest of my life. I will always be alone." The feeling was so frightening and depressing that she broke into tears. She described it to me as a sudden, powerful wave of loneliness. Though she felt that it could have happened to her anywhere, my guess is that her presence at the wake shortly after her own father's death triggered the sense of loneliness.

Because loneliness is a feeling, it is neither good nor bad, neither moral nor immoral. It is human. Loneliness can lead to discouragement and even despair and suicide, but it need not. It might lead to insight, to deeper understanding, to more realistic living, to more unselfish loving. We can't always control feelings; we can control the decisions and choices we make because of our feelings. The feeling of loneliness can crush us, but it need not.

The thesis of this book is that loneliness can be interpreted as a call to and for love. However, before relating loneliness to loving, loneliness should be looked at more closely. That can be done by considering loneliness as a death experience.

Chapter Two

Loneliness and Death

There is no human experience that frightens us so much as death. Rightly so. The specter of death raises all the important questions. What, if anything, does my life mean? Is there any goal or purpose to my life? Is all human existence merely "sound and fury signifying nothing"?

One of the basic errors of which many of us are guilty in relation to death is that we think of death merely in terms of physical causes. Death means heart attacks or cancer or pneumonia. I wish to stress that the death of people will never have any significance or meaning from which hope can be drawn as long as our understanding of death is confined to physical causes.

An example may be the clearest way of making the point. Imagine that, late one night my pet gorilla and I are watching a late movie on TV called *The Bride of Frankenstein Marries a Teenage Werewolf*. Both the gorilla and I have weak hearts. The next morning we are found dead. The doctor proclaims: "It's uncanny. Father Lauder and his gorilla had the same death."

If the doctor is speaking literally, he is wrong. He would have reduced death to its biological or physical causes. My point is that my death is a human death. My death is mine. If anyone is going to explore the meaning of my death then he will have to explore the meaning of a "me," of a human being, of a person. What is the meaning of me? Who am I? Whatever can be said about the meaning of me will illuminate the meaning of my death.

To catch the importance of the point I am trying to make, the role of freedom must be stressed. At any moment of my adult life I am whom I have decided to be. By choosing freely I am constantly creating myself, making myself into the person I wish to be. At any moment of my life it can be said that the person I am is the sum total of the free actions I have performed.

If this emphasis on freedom is kept in mind then we can say that the meaning of my death depends much more on my freedom than on the particular physical causes of my death or on the circumstances that surround my death. How I die or what I die of is relatively unimportant. *Who* dies is of maximum importance.

"Death Experiences"

Anyone who chooses to write about death is at an obvious disadvantage: he has never gone through the experience about which he is writing. Because of that obstacle no one is going to be able to illuminate completely the meaning of death. However, there are some experiences which seem to shed light on that most feared human event. Generally when we speak of a death experience we mean physical death that terminates a person's life. However, there are other death experiences. All experiences of pain and suffering, for example, can be called "death experiences" because they participate in death and foreshadow our death. All such experiences are signs that a person is moving toward death; all point toward the limitation of human persons; all illustrate that persons are not completely in control of their lives. Even a simple reality such as a headache calls attention to our vulnerability, our weakness, our lack of control.

The experience of physical pain is a death experience. We don't like to recall pain or to recognize our fragility. What was the greatest physical suffering of your life? What was the greatest pain you endured? If I ask that question of myself, I find it difficult to answer. It seems to be a law of psychology that we try to block out from memory unpleasant experiences. We seem to try to bury them beyond the memory's capacity of recall. We hope that we will never endure extreme physical pain again.

One of the most frightening aspects of a death experience is that we are relatively helpless before it. Wishing will not make pain disappear. Our inability to control pain merely by our will is a foreshadowing of the inevitability of our death. We are moving toward death whether we wish to do so or not.

The experience of mental anxiety and mental suffering is a good example of a death experience. The most useless advice in the world is: "Don't worry," to a person who is worrying. If the person could stop worrying so easily he or she would not need our two words of advice to help. The torture of anxiety reveals to us that we are not in total possession of our consciousness and our emotional life. The tyranny of anxiety makes our movement toward death more real to us.

Perhaps the strongest death experience is the experience of loneliness. If experienced with great intensity, the feeling might lead to suicide.

All death experiences can narrow a person, can cause a person to be preoccupied with himself.

The death experiences that I have mentioned seem to have special power to make us self-centered. They can make our world smaller. In that sense they are analogous to a physical death that is prolonged and painful. The slow movement of a person fatally ill toward death can appear to be a gradual narrowing of the person's interests and concerns. The person's relations with the world and with other people become fewer and seemingly less intense. The gradual loss of life appears to be a narrowing, a gradual loss of personal presence. In the final hours of such an illness, the invalid's attention and interest may be focused only on the life-sapping sickness. The whole notion of a death experience seems to signal a narrowness and eventual destruction of what it means to be a person.

Death experiences seem to signal this but they need not. This book is based on the belief that loneliness can lead into more profound personal living.

Many of us because of fear try to avoid the questions posed by death. What is paradoxical about this is that death may be the most fruitful and illuminating experience we can consider in our efforts at finding meaning and adopting a hopeful outlook on human life. It would seem that we cannot either discover or give a meaning to life unless we give a meaning to death. This has been well expressed by Nicholas Berdyaev, the Russian existentialist-personalist philosopher. Berdyaev wrote:

> Death is the most profound and significant fact of life: it lifts the very least of mortals above the greyness and banality of life. And only the fact of death puts the question of life's meaning in all its depth. Life in this world has meaning only because there is death: if there were no death in our world, life would be de-

prived of meaning. Meaning is linked with
ending. And if there were no end, if in our
world there was evil and endlessness of life,
there would be no meaning to life whatever.
The meaning of man's moral experience
throughout his whole life lies in putting him
into a position to comprehend death.

I agree with Berdyaev completely. Death provides a bracket for life and that bracket enables us
to consider what the meaning of life is. If there
were no bracket, if there were no ending to life and
yet evil existed then it would be impossible to discover any comprehensive meaning to life. Death
enables us to take a stance on life, to view life as a
unit, as a limited reality that can be explored. It
also enables us to understand loneliness.

There are people who at least for some period
of time in their lives do not seem to take death
seriously. During the so-called "secular 1960's"
one of the characteristics attributed to large groups
of people in this country was a disinterest in the
subject — not just lack of belief in life after death,
but disinterest in the question of whether death
was the end of human existence. Though people
can seem disinterested in the reality of death,
eventually the specter of death intrudes and forces
the person to take some stance toward death.
Whatever stance is taken colors a person's entire
life.

An experience that can underline the power of
death to force persons to ask ultimate questions
is the experience of a wake. Whether the deceased
is a nine-year-old or a 90-year-old, death rocks the
mourners. The question "Why?" naturally arises.
Death seems to be a mistake, an error. It's as
though something became fouled up in the evolu-
tionary process. Plants and animals die and that
seems natural, but not persons; persons shouldn't
die. Shakespeare's King Lear articulated a universal

human reaction to death when with his dead
daughter in his arms he said:

> No, no, no life!
> Why should a dog, a horse, a rat have life,
> And thou no breath at all? (Act 5, Scene 3).

A brilliant piece of art exploring loneliness as a
death experience is Sydney Lumet's film, *The
Pawnbroker,* based on Edward Lewis Wallant's
novel. Formerly a professor of philosophy in Ger-
many, Sol Nazerman (beautifully played by Rod
Steiger) was, with his family, subjected to the most
horrible sorts of torture in a Nazi concentration
camp. Throughout the film short flashbacks indi-
cate some of these tortures. Nazerman's wife,
children and parents eventually were killed by the
Nazis. Though everyone he loved was killed,
Nazerman continued to live. Having become totally
cynical and full of despair, Nazerman stumbles
through life like a dead man. He wants to die. His
only apparent interest is to make money but actually even this interest is feigned.

A person who begins to stir some human
response in Nazerman is his assistant in the pawnshop, a young Puerto Rican boy named Jesus. As
the plot develops, Nazerman, who wants to avoid
all interpersonal relationships because of the pain
they cause, begins to find himself responding
humanly. He is terribly afraid. The horrible memories of what happened in the concentration camp
to those he loved has made the pawnbroker
afraid of ever caring about anyone. To love is to be
vulnerable. At the climax of the film some young
hoodlums break into the shop in order to rob
the safe. They have a gun and warn Nazerman that
if he does not open the safe they will shoot him.
This is exactly what Nazerman wants. He prefers
death to being involved personally with people. As
one of the young hoodlums pulls the trigger to

shoot Nazerman, the young assistant, Jesus, leaps
in front of the pawnbroker and catches the bullet.
The young boy, bleeding and dying, staggers out
of the shop and falls on the sidewalk. Nazerman
is overcome as he kneels by the dying boy. Once
again he feels the horrible pain of losing someone
he loves. Once again he is part of the human race.
The death of Jesus has called Nazerman to life.

At this point in the film the cinematic technique
is particularly striking. Nazerman goes back into
the shop and stands behind the screen that has
separated him from his customers throughout the
film. He seems to be in a cage. In a series of quick,
short flashbacks we see the faces of all the people
who have entered Nazerman's shop, yearning for
a little human concern, starving for a little human
kindness. Interspersed with these flashbacks are
flashbacks of the concentration camp, showing the
horrors that were inflicted on Nazerman and his
family by the Nazis. Nazerman sees clearly that he
has been acting toward the people who entered his
shop just as the Nazis acted toward him and his
family. He looks down at the sticker that contains
all the unredeemed pawn tickets. A number of
times in the film, Nazerman very mechanically
accepted an article to be pawned, tore a pawn
ticket in half, gave one half to the customer and
placed the other on this sticker. All the unredeemed
tickets represent the lives of all the people who
have come to the pawnbroker for help. Remembering the horrors inflicted on him and his family
and remembering the pleading faces of all those
who have come to him for help, Nazerman raises
his hand high into the air and jams it onto the
sticker. There is a closeup of the sticker coming
through Nazerman's hand and the image strongly
resembles that of a crucified hand. By jamming his
hand on the sticker containing all the unredeemed
tickets, Nazerman symbolically identifies himself
with all the broken people who have come to him

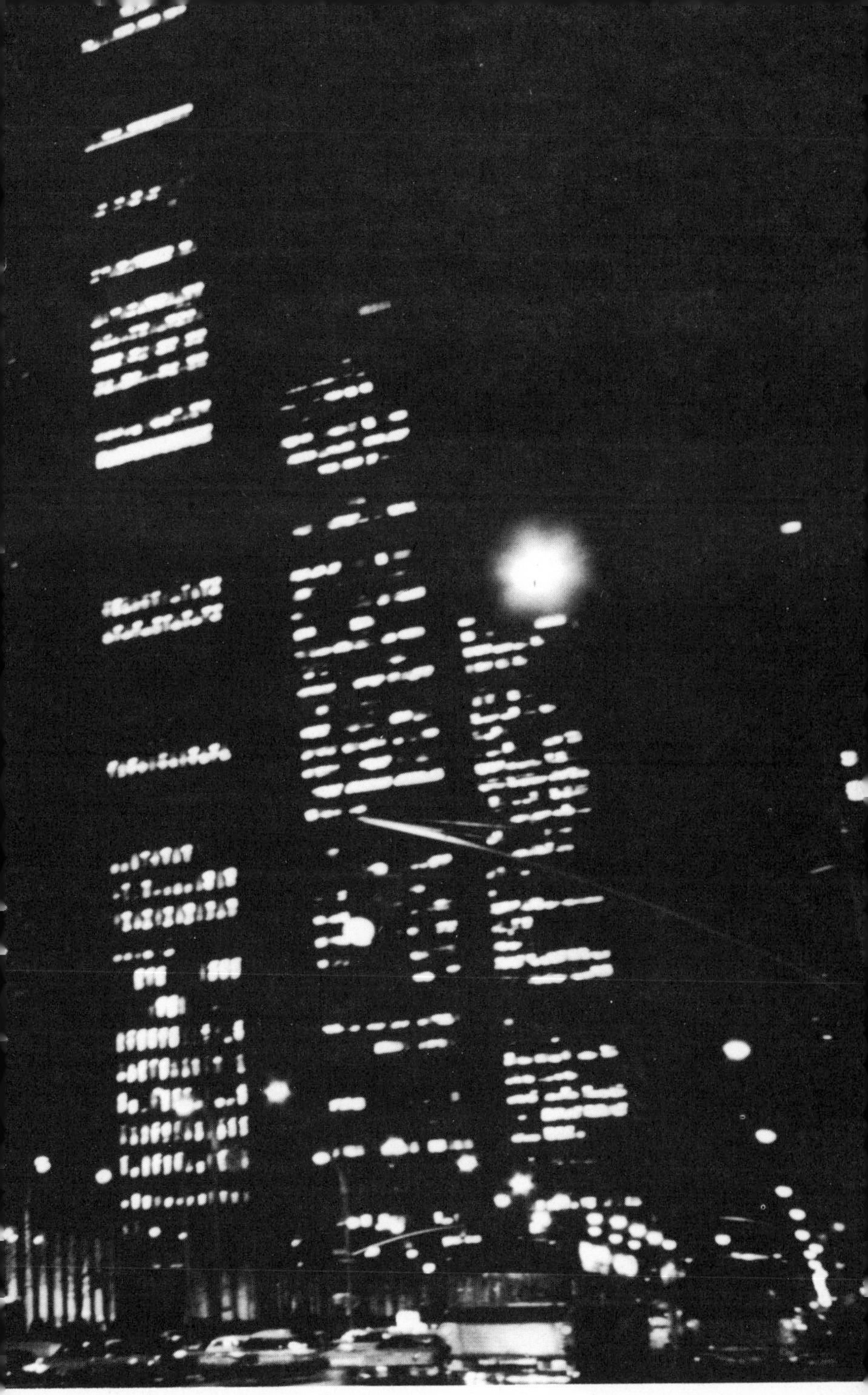

for help. Through his concern for Jesus, Nazerman has begun to live again. As the film comes to a close, Nazerman staggers out from behind the cage and out of the pawnshop. The final shot of the film shows him walking out into the street past the crowd that has gathered around the dead boy.

Though an initial reaction to the film might see the ending as sad and even despairing, the ending is really hopeful. Never again will Sol Nazerman surrender to loneliness. As Nazerman leaves the pawnshop, walks through the crowd of people gathered around the dead Jesus, he is suffering terribly, but he has risen from his loneliness and come back to life and love.

Some social commentators have pointed out that contemporary Americans seem to be battling loneliness by increasing the amount of things they possess. Whether loneliness leads us to raid the refrigerator late at night or buy a more expensive and flashier car than our neighbor, we eventually will lose our battle with loneliness if we center our lives on things. No thing, no matter how expensive or precious, no matter how rare or prized, can fulfill a person. There is in the center of a person an emptiness, if you like, a "nothing," that no thing can ever fill. The needs that a person has go way beyond what things can provide. By trying to combat loneliness with things, a person may be actually increasing loneliness.

This is related to one of the great dangers of present-day advertising. Aren't most commercials on television telling us that we will be happy if we possess some object? The claims that some advertisers make are so extreme that they seem laughable. However, they must work or the advertisers would not spend such enormous sums of money on the gimmick or gimmicks they're using. If the television commercials and other forms of advertising were to be believed, the meaning of person that would be accepted would be a seemingly bottomless pit whose value increases according to the amount of things owned. The value of a person is based on the person's possessions. Buy this car or this suit or this perfume or this mouthwash and you will be a better person. The truth is that things can help us very little in our battle with loneliness and death. Our standpoint on death is central to our standpoint on life and loneliness. Both our standpoint on death and our standpoint on life involve belief, acts of faith.

We say people die. Obviously, everyone undergoes some experience or event that is commonly called death. The key question is what is the meaning of death. A secular culture says death means the end of the person. The only survival that a secular culture will allow a dead individual is in the deeds he accomplished before death or in the memory of those who knew him before he died. For the secularist, there are no other possibilities. Most theistic believers have traditionally claimed that individuals survive death in some other, more important way. They have claimed that individuals personally live after the experience of death. What is absolutely crucial is to see that both the secularist outlook on death and the theistic outlook on death are beliefs. Both outlooks require acts of faith. Both the secularist and the theist look at persons and believe something about what death means. Neither the secularist nor the theist has access to facts that are lacking to the other. Both look at the facts and reach opposite conclusions.

What is the fact of death? To put the matter simply, the fact of death is that an individual's heart stops beating and his brain waves stop functioning. A doctor looks at such an individual and says "he is dead." All that the doctor as a doctor can mean is that the physical signs that we associate with human life are no longer present. The next person to be contacted is the undertaker so that the corpse may be dealt with according to the practices of a particular society.

No one claims that a person whose heart and brain waves have stopped is alive in exactly the same way that he was when both were functioning. The secularist looks at the evidence that the medical doctor offers him and makes an act of faith that the person no longer lives. The point to be stressed is that the secularist makes an act of faith, that he believes something about death. He goes beyond the evidence and believes something that cannot be proven by the evidence available. The doctor as doctor can say nothing about personal immortality.

The Christian listens to the doctor and accepts the facts. These facts show that the person is not alive in the way he was previously. The theist believes from the evidence of the experience of personal living that persons don't cease to exist because hearts stop beating or brain waves cease. Once the secularist and the Christian realize that each lives by faith, honest dialogue can begin. How you interpret physical death can greatly influence your view of loneliness.

Death in Philosophy

Two great personalist philosophers, the Catholic Gabriel Marcel and the Jewish Martin Buber, had beautiful insights into the meaning and mystery of person. Their insights can be very helpful in our efforts to make sense of loneliness.

Marcel made a distinction between having and being. Having is the possession of something external to and separate from the self. A person can manipulate what he or she has and also can transmit it to others. Being does not refer to what is external and separate from the self but rather to a mystery which encompasses the self. Being

refers to the realm of value. Whether a person
responds to life with hope or despair is never
totally due to what is external to the self. To
respond hopefully, a person must tap the rich resources of being in which the person participates;
when a person responds with despair it means
that the person is closed to the values inherent in
the mystery of being. To love would be a matter of
being rather than having.

Buber claimed that there are two kinds of
relationships that a person can have: the I-It and
the I-Thou. The first is a pragmatic, functional
relationship. If a person relates to a thing or even
to another person in terms of I-It, that means that
he or she wishes to use the other. Though I-It
relationships are necessary for human life, if an
individual has only I-It relationships then that
individual will never grow to the fullness of being
a person. An I-Thou relationship is not pragmatic,
functional or utilitarian. The individual from the
center of his or her person encounters the other at
the center of his or her person. Through such relationships, whether they be brief or for a lifetime,
persons grow and develop.

Loneliness cannot be handled or cured on the
level of what Marcel called having or Buber called
I-It. To pursue personal fulfillment on the level of
having or on the level of an I-It may be actually
to increase loneliness. Emphasizing having may
increase your sense of not counting, of being
totally alone, of not really mattering to anyone. No
thing that a person possesses will ever fulfill the
most radical needs of that person. Multiplying I-It
relationships, especially I-It relationships with other
persons, is not only to lock other persons in boxes,
not only to confine and restrict others, but also to
prevent yourself from growing. One of the key
reasons that loneliness is becoming more and more
of a serious problem in our society is that the
levels of having and I-It are so encouraged. This is

one of the dangers of a consumer society. Without
realizing it, people can take their self-image from
advertising and the mass media and judge their
personal worth in terms of the number and price
of the things they own. To value themselves
through things is to court loneliness. If loneliness
can be understood and fruitfully handled, it must
happen on the level of being and on the level of
an I-Thou relationship.

The full meaning of loneliness and the possibilities for good or ill that loneliness has built into
it can be seen by imagining a life ending. Imagine
a terminally ill patient in a hospital room. From
many perspectives that person's world has shrunk
terribly. All the years of living, all the varied experiences, all the plays seen, books read, people
encountered have been reduced to the four walls
of a hospital room. All the dreams and desires for
the future have been stymied by the inevitable
arrival of death. The sick person's world seems
enclosed within the four walls of the hospital room;
the sick person's future is death. If there is any
human experience or situation which would foster
the feeling of not mattering or of not being significant, this is that experience. If there is any meaning, any hope, any antidote to loneliness, it must
be accessible to the terminally ill patient within
that room and with death approaching.

All Terminally Ill
The reason for using the imagined hospital room
situation is to point out that each and every one of
us is in essentially the same situation as the
terminally ill patient. Death may be reaching the
patient more rapidly than it reaches us; our worlds
may seem wider than the four walls of a hospital
room, but no matter how wide, ultimately there
are "walls" around all worlds. No matter how many
distractions we conjure up to deceive ourselves,
each of us is essentially like the patient on the

hospital bed. If the person on the hospital bed cannot hope, then none of us can hope; if the person on the hospital bed cannot find a meaning that liberates from loneliness, then no one can find such a meaning; if the feeling of not mattering, of not counting, of not being significant is an accurate interpretation of the human situation for the person on the hospital bed, then it is an accurate interpretation for every person.

Each of us has to confront death in all its forms — physical, psychological, emotional and spiritual. In any death experience and in any loneliness experience, there are always at least two possibilities, two possible ways of confronting the situation. The one is to surrender to death and judge that it is the end, or to accept the feeling of loneliness, judge that a person really is totally alone and surrender to the despair that probably will follow. The other possibility is to refuse to judge that death is what it seems to be or that the feeling of loneliness must be interpreted to mean that a person is totally alone and not significant. To surrender to death is ultimately cowardly; to believe that you don't matter is to miss the mystery of person.

I once knew a girl who was dying in a cancer hospital. She told me that once the final tests had been taken she wanted to be transferred to a Catholic hospital. She did not want to die in the secular hospital. She wanted to die in an atmosphere in which she could see priests and nuns. She said that just seeing nuns walking around the hospital room would cheer her up. What was the dying girl saying? She wanted to end her life in surroundings that underlined the most important meaning in her life. The nuns and the priests would be signs to her of the truth that death is not the final word. As she confronted death she wanted signs that would support her.

There are a number of signs that can help us as

we confront death and loneliness. One of the strongest signs is the experience of loving and being loved. The experience of loving is so strong that Gabriel Marcel claimed that when you love a person you discover that the person will not die. Love discovers a truth that science could not discover. Love unveils a truth that might remain hidden to those who do not love. What love discovers is that persons are not destroyed by death. The doctor may claim that the heart and brain waves have stopped, the undertaker may bury the mortal remains. The lover knows that somehow the beloved lives.

Love and Death

Is Marcel right? To appreciate an answer the question must be put sharply. Human life is a battle between love and death. Some profound contemporary philosophers such as Jean Paul Sartre and Albert Camus have seen this clearly. Contemporary artists often see and depict the battle clearly for us. Any of the important films of the cinematic genius of Ingmar Bergman can be interpreted as a dramatization of the battle between love and death. Particularly interesting because it poses the problem so starkly is Bergman's *The Seventh Seal* (1957).

The plot of the film concerns a knight, who with his squire, is returning from 10 years in the Crusades. As the film opens Death appears to the knight. There is a terrible plague throughout the land. Death has come to take him but the knight, fighting for time in order to perform some actions that will make his life significant, persuades Death to play a game of chess. The challenge interests Death and he agrees. As the film develops the game of chess is resumed from time to time when the knight pauses in his journey home. As the knight and the squire continue their journey people join them for varying reasons. Among these people are two members of a traveling group of actors, Joseph and Mary, and their infant son, Michael.

To give the plot in outline form is to suggest almost nothing of the subtlety of themes or the power and beauty of cinematic images which Bergman presents. The journey, of course, is not merely the journey home after the Crusades but the journey of life on which man is trying to find a home, a place of security, meaning and significance. Set in the Middle Ages, it is really depicting contemporary man's battle with loneliness.

The title of the film comes from the Book of Revelation (8:1). The seventh seal is the last to be broken by the Lamb in the apocalyptic book of scripture and its breaking causes a silence to follow in heaven for about the space of half an hour. This period of silence Bergman sees as man's opportunity to try to explore and understand the meaning of life. Before dying the knight and all of us must discover some significance, some meaning that makes life worthwhile.

The journey theme is well depicted in this film (and in all of Bergman's films) by frequent shots of the knight and squire on their journey. The viewer almost never sees them in the course of the film at rest. Man is a sojourner, a wanderer, one who has no place to lay his head.

The one occasion in the film when the knight seems to be at rest is one of the most beautiful scenes in Bergman and also an extremely significant scene which sheds light on the relationship between loneliness, love and death. The scene takes place on a lovely sunny day. The knight has just met Joseph and Mary with their little child. Commentators have pointed out that this family is evocative of the Holy Family. Earlier in the film Joseph has said that his son will perform the one impossible trick. His son will throw a ball in the air and succeed in suspending it there. It would seem that this "trick," the suspension of the laws of the universe, would be proper only to a divine being and therefore the baby is some type of Christ-figure.

Sitting on the hillside with the couple and their child, the knight is overcome by the depth of the love between Joseph and Mary and also by the beauty of the day. Receiving some milk and strawberries (the latter is often a symbol of love in Bergman) from the couple, the knight for a second raises the bowl of milk and strawberries almost in an offering or elevation gesture similar to a priest's action at Mass. A moment later he says

> I shall remember this moment. The silence, the twilight, the bowls of strawberries and milk, your faces in the evening light. . . . I'll carry this memory between my hands as carefully as if it were a bowl filled to the brim with fresh milk. And it will be an adequate sign — it will be enough for me.

It is important to note that the one significant act that the knight eventually performs is to save Joseph, Mary and the child from dying by distracting Death during one segment of the chess game. Of all the important characters in the film the two are the only people who do not die. Bergman seems to be hinting or suggesting that somehow love conquers both death and loneliness. But does it and, if so, how? To answer, some explanation of the mystery of loving is required.

Loving and being loved also sheds light on the meaning of loneliness. To be a person is to be radically needy. If our need for others is not met, the experience of loneliness can be devastating. The great contribution that the experience of loneliness can make to our personal living is that it can help us see our need to love and to be loved.

Chapter Three

Loneliness and Loving

The feeling of loneliness can be interpreted to mean that each of us is alone in an unfriendly universe. Sometimes the feeling can be so strong that this seems to be the only meaning it can have. Yet it isn't really what loneliness means at all. It's the wrong interpretation of the feeling. What loneliness can reveal to us is our most radical need, our deepest drive, our most important desire. Loneliness tells us that to be a person we must love and be loved. Without loving and being loved we are hopelessly alone. What could be a benevolent universe becomes a hellhole.

That the feeling we don't matter to anyone should bother us suggests that we *ought* to matter. The feeling of loneliness suggests that life ought not to be like this, that a person ought not to be totally alone. I recall a brief period in my life when I felt terribly alone. For two and a half years I had been rushing through my graduate work because I wanted to have a doctorate by the time the college seminary was opened. Having begun study in the fall of 1964 and knowing that the seminary

would open in the fall of 1967, I pushed myself
very hard over a three-year period. As I was
coming into the homestretch, one of the last
hurdles I had was the oral doctoral comprehensives.
Having finished all the course work I spent a
couple of months studying for "comps," which
were scheduled for January 6. I went home for
Christmas but decided to return to the university
a day or two after Christmas to spend the last 10
days or so studying. My friends told me I should
enjoy the Christmas vacation but I was afraid:
I had been pressing very hard and I didn't want to
trip on one of the last hurdles. I returned to the
university. Almost no one was around. It was a
cold, dark period and all my surroundings seemed
bleak. The university cafeteria was closed and
so I had dinner every night in a diner. I recall
looking around the diner at the people, most of
whom were old and must have been without
families and I thought, I only have to do this for
a week or two. What must it be like to eat here
every night? What must it be like to have no family
or real home and be forced each evening to take
your main meal in a diner? I remember feeling
alone and very lonely. Once again I wondered,
as I feared failing the test, whether the goal was
worth all the sacrifices I had to make. In preparing
for the comprehensives during these two weeks
I learned a great deal more than the material I was
studying. I learned how loneliness can plague
people and how blessed those people are who in
their home are surrounded by those who love them.

Love Is Creative

Part of the cure for loneliness is to be loved.
The experience of being loved, of knowing that
someone cares for you, that you matter to someone is the greatest antidote to loneliness. The
expression, "What being-loved makes being-do is
precisely to be" (Frederick Wilhelmsen, *The Meta-*

physics of Love) has a great deal of insight. All
creatures are because of God's love. From nothing-
ness God's love has called creatures into existence.
Stones are because of God's love, trees are because
of God's love, mountains and rivers and lakes are
because of God's love. The entire physical universe is a product of God's love. The physical
universe is beautiful because of God's love. His
love let it be: "What being-loved makes being-do
is precisely be."

Persons are because of God's love. There are
growth and development within the physical universe, and there can be growth within the world
of persons. The statement, "What being-loved
makes being-do is precisely be," achieves its most
profound illustration among persons. Every person is, but he is also "not yet"; every person
exists, but has not yet reached the fullness of personal existence. Many realities feed into the
development of a person, for example, various
experiences and educational opportunities, but
the greatest aid toward personal growth is being
loved. In a way that applies to no other activity,
love is creative of person. God's love calls persons
into existence. Love helps persons develop. Each
of us needs to be loved if we are going to learn
how to love.

Distance from those who love us and whom we
love can intensify feelings of loneliness. A dear
friend of mine had to be separated from her hus-
band and year-old daughter for almost two
years. While they returned to their home in Korea,
she had to remain in this country to finish her
studies. People who did not know her well
thought that she took this separation rather easily
and painlessly. Her carefree appearance and
charming outgoing personality probably contributed
to that impression. However, to know her well
was to know that at times her loneliness became
almost unbearable. Though I know my friendship

eased her loneliness she would in moments of
extreme loneliness say, "I have no one, no one. I
am all alone." The physical distance between her
and her family and the pain my friend experienced
because of it underlined for me the need at the
center of our personhood for love. What also
underlined this need was my realization that the
physical distance between her and her family was
merely the occasion for the intensification of my
friend's loneliness. Perhaps the most sensitive
person I know, my friend confessed to me that she
believed the experience of loneliness could never
be completely overcome. The strongest human
loves can't destroy loneliness totally. My friend
existentially experienced what I have come to believe largely through philosophical and theological
reflection, that on this side of the grave loneliness
will never be completely erased from personal
existence. Even when physical distance is overcome there can never be too much loving.

Invitation to Grow

The experience of being loved includes within
it the invitation to growth. When a person is loved
he or she is invited to become a new person. By
accepting the love of the lover, the beloved can
achieve a new fullness, a new richness, a new depth
of being. Nothing but the experience of being
loved can supply this unique opportunity for
growth, this extraordinary opportunity to be created. A person can read numerous books and this
experience might bring about a profound change;
a person can travel around the world and this
experience might provide an enormous broadening
of vision; a person might attend the great univer-
sities, achieve numerous degrees, and this might
provide a deepening of insight. However, nothing
can change a person the way the experience of
being loved can.

"What being-loved makes being-do is precisely

be." Being loved, if the love is accepted by the one loved, can heal the beloved's wounds, smooth off the rough edges of the personality, enable the person to move with courage into the future. Of course if the beloved does not accept the love of the lover, then the beloved does not grow through that particular love. Indeed, if the beloved does not accept the love of the lover, it is possible that the beloved will move toward isolation. Love seems to be a grace, a gift, and the beloved by refusing the gift of love is refusing a unique chance to grow. When love enters a human life it seems to be an existential moment: once love has been offered nothing is the same. Either the person says yes to the gift of love which means growth or no which may mean decline.

Possibility of Confusion

The greatest antidote for loneliness, therefore, is to be loved. But there is a catch. Once we are aware of the importance of love in our lives, there is a danger of trying to make ourselves superficially lovable. It is the need to be loved that advertising plays on — use this mouthwash, or buy this car, or wear this bra, and you will be lovable!

Every individual, because each is a person, is lovable. An "unlovable person" is a contradiction in terms. To be a person is to be a call for love and to be worthy of love. Of course there is nothing wrong with "putting your best foot forward" or "coming out of your shell" and making yourself more attractive. The danger is that a person will confuse some physical attraction or characteristic with what makes the person lovable. A person is lovable because he or she is a unique person, one of God's masterpieces.

One of the marvelous things about love is that it focuses in on the you. The lover always says, at least implicitly, "I love you because you are you." This is why the Christian commandment that we

love all people is quite reasonable: in spite of un-
attractive characteristics all persons are lovable.

If every person is lovable, and if there is a
danger in trying to change certain external appearances because we may deceive ourselves into
thinking that the assumed qualities or characteristics are what make us lovable, is there nothing
that we can do, no action that we can take, to combat loneliness directly? Is there nothing we can do
but wait for people to love us? There is something that we can do. With the exception of being
loved, it is the most fulfilling human activity. It
is the most "personal" act that an individual can
do. We have been discussing being loved as an
antidote to loneliness. We must now discuss loving.

Loving Is Relating

To love someone is to come out of yourself,
to step outside yourself, in a sense, to give yourself
away. The essence or nature of person is to be
relational. There are hundreds of ways of relating,
and a person can decide which way or ways will be
chosen. The most important, the most profound,
the most personal way, is to love.

Once an individual discovers that other persons
are in need of love and are lovable, a kind of
challenge is present. Should the individual respond? A response will mean going out of yourself, surrendering yourself, sacrificing yourself. It
will mean a kind of dying, but it will also mean a
new kind of living. Those who love testify to this.
Human experience reveals that we are never more
ourselves than when we are loving. Though deep
love may be the most difficult human activity, perhaps as difficult as grave sin, it is also the most
marvelous experience. We are never better than
when we are loving. It's paradoxical, but the best
way to overcome our own loneliness is to be concerned about the loneliness of others. To appreciate our own worth, we ought to appreciate the

worth of others. The best way of attacking our
own loneliness is to attack the loneliness of others.

Loving Is Choosing

Though loneliness is a feeling, love is not a feeling. To proclaim through popular songs, films and
other mass media that love is a feeling may be
the most serious heresy of our society. Love is
often accompanied by feelings, but love itself is not
a feeling. The expression "falling in love" is not
accurate. We may fall into feelings but we don't
fall in love. We choose to love. We decide whom
we will love. When a love becomes especially intense we may "fall into feelings" that are so
strong that they overcome us. The feelings may
blind us, but love is not blind. Love helps persons
to see. Lovers see what others cannot see.

Love can be expressed in the words, "I am for
you; I am in favor of you; I want to serve you; my
personal presence is for you." Of course, love is
not the saying of the words but the giving of
the self.

Through loving, a person becomes aware of a
new depth in his or her personal existence. A person has a new sense of self. Whatever demands
love makes, whatever sacrifices love leads to, whatever unselfishness love asks, the loving person
becomes aware that this is the secret of personal
living; individuals become persons through giving
themselves away in love.

What a person learns is important for a person's
self-development; what or whom a person loves is
even more important for self-development. The
saying, "Show me your friends and I'll tell you who
you are," is based on a profound insight: in loving,
the lover surrenders himself or herself over to the
beloved and so must be influenced by the beloved.
You are not what you eat; "you are whom you
love" is closer to the truth.

The forms of love are different: the love of friends, the love of marriage partners, the love of priest and parishioners, the love of teacher and student are just a few examples. Different love relationships make different demands on lovers. Universal in all forms of loving is the special presence that the lover provides to those who are loved, the unique gift of self that the lover provides to those loved.

Presence Essential to Love

Loving demands presence. Unless some kind of presence is given, no love exists. The importance of presence can be easily seen when love is in its early stages. The boy begins to date the girl a couple of times a month. Then it's every week. Soon he's at the house so frequently that the girl's father may think that he's gaining a boarder. Finally the boy and girl decide to be so present that they choose to spend the rest of their lives with each other. Loving always involves some kind of presence. This is why lovers exchange gifts and photographs and letters. They are saying in as many ways as they can, "I am for you." The lover wants to be with the beloved.

There are various ways of being present. Personal presence is always different from the way a thing is present. Among the numerous types of personal presence, loving presence is the most healing, not only for the beloved, but for the lover. By being present in love, the lover can conquer the feeling of loneliness; the lover can unveil the lie latent in the feeling that he or she is alone. Marvelous examples of personal creative presence can be observed at an Alcoholics Anonymous meeting. Anyone who has either spoken at length with an alcoholic or attended an Alcoholics Anonymous meeting can see that feelings of loneliness can be a pressing problem for the alcoholic. One of the reasons for the success of A.A. is the strong sense of community that it fosters. The first step toward victory for the alcoholic can be when he realizes that he is not the only person in the world who ever had a problem with alcohol. To know that others have suffered the way you have, but fought and won, can provide tremendous support. If an alcoholic is away from home in a distant city he can find out by a phone call where the nearest A.A. meeting is and by attending it have instant community.

Love Is Free

A person can't force someone to give love, but a person can choose to love. The very choice, the very act of loving reveals that the lover is not alone. The act of loving reveals that the feeling of loneliness is being misread if it is interpreted to mean that the lover is alone. Through loving, a person makes contact; through loving, a person can see his or her importance and significance; through loving, a person can discover that a unique gift can be given only by this person: the gift of self. That gift is more valuable than the entire physical universe. Loving leads the lover to a new sense of self. Even if loneliness disappears it can be seen as having had a special value: loneliness points toward loving. Loneliness leads lovers to love more deeply and more widely.

Rather than trying to gain the characteristics or qualities that advertising proposes to make people more lovable, a person should realize that he or she becomes most lovable by being a lover. The reason is that through loving, a person reveals his or her true self. A person is made to love. By loving, we make more clear the most profound truth about ourselves: we are lovable.

Chapter Four

Loneliness
and Friendship

Any discussion of loneliness and loving would be incomplete without special attention being given to friendship. It is one of the most important keys to both understanding and handling loneliness. Reflecting on friendship I have become aware how precious it is and also how much it costs. In one sense friendship is quite natural and normal. Yet it demands a great deal of time and effort. Attraction may happen between people but friendships are chosen and they must be chosen again and again. The old joke is true: our relatives are given to us but we choose our friends.

Occasionally when I meet a person for the first time I feel a very strong attraction. The person seems to be someone with whom I would like to spend some time, someone to whom I would like to reveal myself, someone with whom I would like to share my ideas. No matter how strong this attraction is, friendship doesn't take place until people allow it to take place. Friendship is a love relationship and all love relationships are chosen.

In my life I have encountered a few people who

seem to relate to everyone in the same way. Such people often have many acquaintances. They know many people and are known by many. Yet, at least the few I have known, don't seem to be known very deeply by anyone. They seem to be experts at being "friendly" without ever letting anyone very close. Sometimes such a person will describe his relationships by saying that he is friends with everyone. Unfortunately, this probably means that he has no real friends, no close or intimate friends. It may also mean that he is quite lonely. To have friends usually demands time and effort. Often friendship requires a demanding kind of presence. Friendship costs something but friendship is well worth the price.

The old axiom is true: "Show me your friends and I'll tell you who you are." I don't think it means that your friends must have personalities similar to yours or even have tastes similar to yours. I'm crazy about movies but some of my closest friends don't like them and don't go to them. Friendship, however, does demand a sharing, a deep sharing. When the sharing disappears I think the friendship disappears.

Friends are people who "hear us" on a deeply personal level. Human life can be examined in terms of hearing and responding. Hearing requires some amount of giving on the part of the listener. Persons who cannot listen deeply may be persons who are prevented from listening because of some personal problem. Really listening requires a kind of self-possession, a kind of freedom. To listen profoundly to someone requires that the listener be in control of himself to some extent, that the listener is able to be still and not preoccupied with himself or with what he is going to say when the speaker is finished. Perhaps Jesus was partly alluding to this when he said to Martha, "You are busy about many things but only one thing is necessary. Mary has chosen the better part." When a person really listens to us, when a person is profoundly present to us, we often have the sense of being healed and freed. This is one reason why the mere process of confessing can be a healing process. I tell someone that I am a sinner, that I have done wrong, that I am ashamed of myself, and yet that other does not condemn me but is receptively present to me. That listening presence can heal my wounds.

The person who really listens also helps me toward freedom because I am allowed to come out of myself, I am allowed to leave behind what is tying me in knots, what is restricting me. A friend helps me to be unlocked, to be released. A friend calls me from my loneliness. A friend supports me as I try to face the future courageously. A friend, by hearing me, helps me to respond not only to him but to life. Someone without friends may not yet be a person.

Openness Essential

How do friendships begin? Of the many people I encounter why does friendship happen with some and not with others? Is it some physical characteristic of the other that appeals to me and draws me into a friendship? I suppose that accounts for the beginning of some friendships, but even more basic and more essential is the willingness or openness that a person must have if a friendship is going to happen. An example from my own life may set off memories from your past and remind you how some of your friendships began.

When I was a graduate student at Marquette, I was on a very tight schedule because I had a limited amount of time in which to get a doctorate. Often I avoided entering into relationships with other students because I was pushing myself and had to limit my social life. Because Marquette had no residence for priests, I had my own rooms in an apartment building. Early in the fall of my last

year, while I was in the cafeteria at Marquette
where I ate regularly, I met two girls who had
recently graduated from the university. They told
me that they were soon moving into the apartment
building where I had my apartment and they
invited me to visit them. Each girl's first name
was Sue. Even now I recall thinking, Oh, these
two could be a nuisance — bothering me when
I'm trying to rush toward getting the degree this
year.

A few weeks later, one Saturday morning while
I was writing a paper on the German philosopher,
Friedrich Hegel, the bell rang. I went to the door
and there were the two girls. They explained that
they had moved in and invited me to come and
see how they had decorated their apartment.
Figuring I'd get rid of them and also that I'd make
clear that I had no time to waste with making
friends, I said, "Oh, I'm working on a paper on
Hegel and I have to get it finished." Their faces
dropped. "Oh, we're sorry," they muttered. I
think as I returned to my desk I had mixed feelings,
some of success and some of guilt. Sometime
during that year, I became more human and more
open to friendship because by July the "two Sues"
had become two of my closest friends and they
have remained so until this moment, 10 years later.
When I left Marquette they gave me a book, *On
Christianity: Early Theological Writings* by Hegel,
with the inscription, "For the next time you want
to avoid a friendship." I expect many of us either
consciously or unconsciously avoid friendship because we feel we "don't have the time," but often
what we are doing with time can't compare to the
rich experience of friends. The "two Sues" are
among the beautiful blessings in my life.

To Establish Ties
Retelling this anecdote from my own life
reminds me of a marvelous section from the beau-

tiful and insightful story, *The Little Prince.* In the story the little prince is looking for friends. He comes upon a fox who asks the little prince to tame him. Not knowing what the fox means by "tame" the little prince asks the fox, who explains that it means to establish ties. The fox continues to explain:

"To you, I am nothing more than a fox like a hundred thousand other foxes. But if you tame me, then we shall need each other. To me, you will be unique in all the world. To you, I shall be unique in all the world. . . . Please — tame me!" he said.

"I want to very much," the little prince replied. "But I have not much time. I have friends to discover, and a great many things to understand."

"One only understands the things that one tames," said the fox. "Men have no more time to understand anything. They buy things all ready made at the shops. But there is no shop anywhere where one can buy friendship, and so men have no friends any more. If you want a friend, tame me. . . ."[1]

To have friends is to establish ties. It is to recognize your own needs and the needs of others. It is to recognize your own loneliness and the loneliness of others. I suppose to have friends you have to recognize your vulnerability and allow others to see it. None of us finds this easy, but the richness that friendship can introduce into your life makes the risk not so frightening.

Perhaps the anecdote I told about the "two Sues" will recall to the reader's mind the beginning of some friendship he or she has experienced. There is a mystery to friendship, a depth that cannot be completely analyzed or fully understood. Yet next to friendship most of what people hold dear fades in importance.

---

[1]*The Little Prince,* Antoine de Saint-Exupery, Harcourt Brace Jovanovich, Inc.

Friendship Is Sharing

One of the striking characteristics about any friendship is that the friends share a whole universe of meaning and memories. To observe a long friendship, one that has extended over a number of years, is to observe a unique world that has been forged through much time, much love, and perhaps through much pain. When a third person is with two close friends the individual becomes aware that he or she is sharing an entire world that is common to the two friends. The friends know each other so well that each can anticipate the reactions of the other. A friend often knows you, at least in some areas of your life, better than you know yourself.

One aspect of friendship that particularly interests me is the creativity of friendship. There is one level on which the creativity that two friends exert on one another is obvious. If I like literature then at least indirectly my friend is going to learn about literature and perhaps be motivated to read some literature. My friend will be the beneficiary of my interest and may be influenced by my taste. Each person opens up his or her world of interests to a friend. In this area it can be said that one greatly influences or "creates" the other. Often a friend is heard to say something like, "Until I became friendly with him I was never interested in that topic. He opened up the whole area to me. If it hadn't been for his friendship, I never would have been interested." Such statements suggest the specific kind of influence that friends have on one another.

A more important and a more mysterious kind of creativity is also operative in friendships. Let's take a time of tragedy as an example. At a time of tragedy a friend is a tremendous support. Even the word "support" suggests the kind of creativity that a friend can have. A friend holds us up, lifts us up, helps to prevent us from falling apart. In a moment of tragedy a friend doesn't really have to do anything, but rather has to be somewhere. He or she has to be present to us. What we want in a moment of tragedy is a presence. We want someone who is in favor of us, who is present for us. This is the crucial role that a friend can play at a time of tragedy. The very presence of a friend "creates" us, enables us to get through a difficult situation. At times of tragedy we want our friends with us. They help us to be our best selves, our strongest selves.

What is crucial to the example is the kind of creativity that friends exert all the time. I don't claim to understand this creativity but I have observed it taking place. I really don't think anyone can understand it without completely understanding a human person, and I don't think anyone but God completely understands a human person. It seems as though a little bit of the divine has slipped into human relationships.

In trying to comment on the creative action that one friend can have on another, I will use the word "you" to refer to the core of the person that goes beyond all specific characteristics such as sex, age, weight, occupation and so forth. Real friendship always focuses on the "you" because love focuses on the "you." By focusing on the "you" of a friend, an individual supplies an absolutely unique ingredient for personal growth. It may also be the unique ingredient if loneliness is to be conquered. Through personal presence, through the gift of love in friendship, an individual calls his or her friend to become a deeper "you," or to put it another way, calls the person to transcend the present self and become a new self. What never ceases to amaze me is that this occurs at the level of the "you," not on the level of some specific characteristic. I can create a new "you," I can create my friend into a new being. Of course, I don't do it the way God does it, but I think I come more close in my "friendly presence" to the creative act of God than in any other human activity. Creating artistic masterpieces pales in comparison to the creation of friends.

Of course, the creation of a person by his friend does not happen automatically. The "friendly presence" that an individual offers must be accepted by the friend or else nothing happens. However, if the "friendly presence" is received and accepted, creation takes place. A marvelous gift has been received and one of the great marvels of human living has occurred. There just isn't anything else like friendship. It's at the top of any list of the joys of human living.

I had a crazy experience a couple of years ago that in a special way revealed to me the richness of friendship. I had a chance to go on a winter vacation. In making plans during November and December, it became clear that none of my friends would be able to accompany me. In the midst of a hectic semester the idea of going away alone for five or six days seemed like a good idea. I figured I'd play tennis and swim and with my marvelous personality meet people easily and quickly.

What seemed like a great idea during the wild and woolly work days turned out to be a disaster when put into execution. I went away alone — the water was beautiful, the tennis marvelous and I was miserable. I can't remember ever feeling so lonely. I found myself trying to strike up conversations with strangers, conversations about anything:

"Nice weather, isn't it? Isn't the sun great? Isn't the pool wonderful? I'm down here for a few days' vacation. I teach philosophy. Why are you walking away? Wait! I haven't told you my life story yet. Listen, I'm a rather witty person. Come back, I can be a lot more interesting than I seem!" I found myself tracking down people and trying to impose myself on them. I was pretty down.

How, I wondered, could I have thought it was a
good idea to go on a vacation alone? Eating dinner
alone in the evening was the high point of loneliness and the low point of the day. Though I met
many waiters none of them seemed terribly impressed with me. Though I had planned to go
on vacation for five days I came home after three.

What the experience of the vacation revealed to
me is how much we receive from our friends.
They are constantly healing us, creating us, helping us through the difficult periods of life. The old
Beatle song has a real insight: "I get by with a little
help from my friends." It is easy to observe how
important the presence of friends is when we are
in difficult situations. The strongest of us is fairly
fragile. We bruise easily. Even the most blessed
life has some rough spots in it.

The most dramatic situations are the ones in
which we spot easily the contribution that our
friends make to us. The experience of suffering
and death highlights the richness of friendship. If a
person is in a hospital, just seeing a friend can be
a tremendous boost. To know that someone cares,
that someone is concerned can be a healing experience. No matter what the reason is that you're
in a hospital, the face of a friend is a medicine
that can't be bought.

An even more dramatic instance is the experience of death. It is easy to observe how important
the presence of friends is at a wake or a funeral.
It is not that friends say in words some terribly
important message that speaks to the mourners.
The verbal messages the mourners can speak to
themselves. What matters is the presence of
friends. Their physical presence reveals their love
and concern. Dag Hammarskjold has written,
"Friendship needs no words; it is solitude delivered
from the anguish of loneliness." The personal presence of friends at a wake says, "We know what

you are suffering. We wish we could remove the suffering and the pain and the sorrow. We can't but we're here to show our love." I know that in my experience of mourning those I love, the presence of friends was the greatest kind of gift.

Friends heal us. All of us have hang-ups, emotional problems, idiosyncrasies. Friends smooth off the rough edges of our personality, heal the wounds of our psyche. What a therapist does in an extreme situation when a person needs special help, friends do all the time.

Friends Touch Us

Our parents have the greatest influence on us. I think after them, our friends are the strongest influence on our lives. Institutions, as institutions, can never affect us as profoundly or as intimately as our friends can. Even the great teachers who may have deeply influenced us did so not because of the material they taught but because of themselves. A great teacher really teaches himself. He convinces students because of who he is. As I think of the great teachers I have had, I can remember very little of the content they taught but I remember clearly the tremendous impression they as persons made on me. I think the same can be said of religious leaders. Their person comes through and touches us. Though there were many quotable quotes attributed to Pope John, what really impressed the world was the man himself. The kind of presence that great teachers and leaders communicate in a dramatic way, friends provide daily to us. Friends touch us. The contribution of friends is most obvious when they are absent.

A priest friend of mine tells me that he feels most lonely late at night. He claims that during the day his busyness distracts him from all feelings of loneliness. As he works with people and as he tries to minister to the needs of his parishioners, he never feels lonely. Indeed he often has the opposite feeling: he feels as though more people wish to relate closely to him than he could ever possibly form deep relationships with. But at night when he is alone he begins to have strong feelings of loneliness. His frequent problems with insomnia are probably related to his feelings of loneliness. His busyness during the day distracts him from dealing with a restlessness and lack of ease with himself that emerge strongly at night.

For over 10 years my friend developed a pattern of activity that may have eased his loneliness. Without his awareness the activity may have sprung from his loneliness. He would stay up late night after night with his pastor. They would talk and watch television until two or three in the morning even though my friend might have the 6:30 Mass the next morning. When I asked him to describe the conversations, he would belittle them as small talk and say that he had to start getting to bed earlier. Now in retrospect he sees that these early morning conversations were filling a need: the need not to feel alone. There are similar patterns of activity in most of our lives. Loneliness leads us to harmful patterns of activity more than we usually realize. The absence of friends can encourage feelings of loneliness.

Friends Understand

There is an enormous amount of understanding that colors the relationship between two friends. Because of the time they have spent together, because of the concern and care that they have shared, friends can anticipate one another's attitudes and actions. Often a friend can predict, "He won't enjoy that" or "She'll like this." If someone is asked why his or her friend will react in a certain manner the response, "That's the way he is," contains a whole history of interaction.

When two people become close, there is a strong desire on the part of each that the other develop

to the full all of his or her talents. A person wants
what is best for a friend. It's normal and natural
for one friend to correct another. Part of the beauty
of friendship is that a person can honestly articulate the faults of a friend to the friend's face. But
a person must never put conditions on the love that
is extended to a friend. Love must never have
strings attached. "I love you if you'll change your
way of living", or "I love you as long as you do
what I want you to do" are really not professions
of love at all. Love is always focused on the you.
It goes beyond all conditions and requirements.
Lovers always say, at least implicitly, "I love you
because you are you, not because of anything
you've accomplished, or because you're physically
attractive or because I want to use you, but because
you are who you are." Friendship in the deepest
sense is also focused on the you. It is this focus,
this special personal presence of a friend that provides such tremendous support and encouragement to us in both good times and bad.

There is a fine line between loving the real
person and hoping that the person will change and
overcome some bad habit or habits. Love and
hope for change are quite consonant. However,
what is expressed in the statement, "I love the you
I want you to become," is not real love. A person
can't love the "you I want you to become" because
that "you" does not yet exist and may never
exist. More than any human activity love centers
on the real. The only person who can be loved is
the actually existing person. An individual may
hope that a person changes but if he or she loves
the person, then it is the existing person who is
loved. Though the faults of the person may not
be loved, the person who has faults is loved. This
is one of the great contributions that friends make:
they accept us as we are. Friends may want us to
be better but they accept us as we are. The very
act of acceptance enriches our being. I can believe

that I am worthwhile, that I have value, that I am important if my friend loves me. I can overcome my loneliness if my friend loves me. The act of acceptance helps me to grow and change for the better.

It is the act of acceptance that friends give us that enables us to confide in them. I can't tell strangers what I am really like but I can tell my friend. There is within each of us a need to be real with someone, a desire to communicate our true selves to someone. We can do this with our friends. When we communicate our true selves to our friends we can listen, really listen, to the word that is spoken to us. It may be a word of comfort, a word of consolation, a word of correction, a word of advice, but because it is our friend speaking it is always a word of love. It's a word that can break the chains of loneliness.

To be a human person is to be a creature of growth. What a person relates to and how a person relates either fosters or hinders that growth. The literature we read, the films we see, the places we visit, the people we see, the people we meet contribute to growth or work against growth. Our friends supply what can be obtained nowhere else. No book, no person, no film, no country, no acquaintance can be substituted for a friend.

Sometimes you hear someone describing a friend by saying something like, "He's there when I need him." That expression sums up the meaning of friendship. Though the expression usually refers to some crisis situation, it can be broadened to apply to all aspects of personal living. There is a radical need in each of us to be loved and a friend fills up that need with his or her personal presence. To think you can live without friends is a frightening kind of foolishness. It is to court loneliness.

Friends Not Made

Not ever having read the book, *How to Make Friends and Influence People* by Dale Carnegie, I am far from an expert on its value or on the value of so-called personality courses. I know the words, "How to make friends," turn me off immediately. Images of false appearances, fake joviality and manipulative activity come to mind. We don't make friends. It seems to me that making friends is impossible. As far as I can see, friendship is a gift. There is no way that friends can be made. Things can be made but friends can't. People can be tricked into thinking that they are our friends and people can be used and maneuvered because they think that friendship exists. But read friendship is a gift.

At certain moments in life, for example at Thanksgiving, we recall the many blessings and gifts we have received. High on most lists are parents and health. What is freely given by parents is literally beyond counting. They form and mold in the early years when a child's consciousness is young and the conscience is just dawning; they serve as models until sons and daughters reach adult age and even then their influence continues. The gift of health is most appreciated when it is placed in jeopardy. Even a headache can give us a new appreciation of our health. When we are sick we are amazed at how we have taken our health for granted. How many times have we heard a sick person say, "If I get well, I'll never complain about anything again."

Friendship is one of life's great gifts. It is true that we receive our relatives through our birth but we choose our friends. It is also true that merely choosing individuals as our friends does not make them our friends. A friend must give himself or herself for friendship to happen. A friendship is the result of two free self-gifts.

Just as we, when mature, become aware of the enormous gifts that our parents have given, just as we become aware of the great gift of health when we begin to lose it, so we appreciate friends when they are absent or when we lose them. Often when we are enjoying something we may wish our friends were with us. When we are having a pleasant experience it seems normal to think how much someone we love would enjoy it. When a friend dies we become painfully aware of what a magnificent gift friendship is.

In the early 1960's I lost two dear friends, a priest and a layman, each in his early 30's. Both were outstanding Christians. Each had a profound effect on me when I was in college. During the years of friendship I shared much with each of them and learned much from each. My two friends were outstanding Christian intellectuals and each made real for me the excitement and dignity of the intellectual life. They also revealed to me the special role that a Catholic intellectual can play in the contemporary world. Each of them, as friends do, had a genuine interest in my vocation and education. Each was always interested to hear what I was doing, what books I was reading, what I thought about one or another issue. Though both saw me ordained, each had died before I was sent away by my bishop to study philosophy. Each of my friends was a teacher. Can you guess how many times in the 10 years that I have been teaching I have imagined discussing ideas with them? How often I have wondered what their reaction would be to some of the changes in the Church? I wish I could share my thoughts with them, benefit from their reactions, learn from their wisdom. I miss my friends very much and though I enjoyed their presence while they were alive, I appreciate them even more now.

Friendship Is Free

What makes a gift so attractive is that the giver
is not compelled to give it. Sometimes when a
person is embarrassed or stunned by receiving a
gift he or she will say something like, "Why did
you do that? You didn't have to do that. You
didn't have to give me anything." If the giver
wanted to answer such a comment some statement
like the following would probably be an accurate
description of the situation, "I know I didn't have
to give it. If I were forced, it would not be a gift.
I gave it because I wanted to give you something
that represented my love for you."

Gifts are signs of the giver. That's probably
why often it is difficult to pick a gift. The more
special the person who will receive it, the more
difficult the giver's task in choosing the gift. Friendship is the greatest gift: in it what is given is the
self.

Priestly Friendships

I know of no profession in which a person can
meet someone for a brief period of time and yet
relate so deeply as in the priesthood. I could
recount numerous examples from my own life.
Any priest could. Imagine a priest making hospital
visitations. He comes upon a person who has a
terminal disease. He may know very little about
the person's background or the specific characteristics of the individual's personality. But very
quickly the priest and the patient can relate on a
very profound level. First of all, whoever the priest
is, he represents to the patient a whole world of
meaning that is central to the person, especially
now that the person is facing death. Whoever the
patient is, he or she is someone immediately confronting the mystery of death, a mystery that the
priest has dedicated his life toward confronting,
making sense of, relating to the meaning of religion. In a matter of seconds the priest and patient

can bypass a whole set of conventions and customs that are usually followed when friendships develop. The priest and the patient can encounter each other at the most profound level and this can happen very rapidly. Perhaps they will never see each other again. Yet, if the encounter is genuine both will have been changed for eternity.

Such meetings can happen often in a priest's life. My hunch is that they don't occur often in other people's lives. Within a priest's experience such meetings can occur in the rite of reconciliation, at a wake, in the office and, indeed, almost anywhere. They can occur in as unlikely a place as a subway. I suspect the reason such encounters happen in a priest's life is tied to the meaning, mystery and mission of the priesthood. Whatever the individual priest's virtues or vices, talents or weaknesses, there are numerous situations in which he can be met solely and precisely because he is a servant of the Word or, to use language more familiar to some, a "man of God."

In the usual meaning of the word "friendship" the encounters I've been referring to cannot really be called friendships. Though the priest may be meeting the person on a very deep level, the relationship wouldn't usually be described as a friendship. Such meetings might be more profound than many friendships, or might be less valuable than other friendships, but certainly there's a kind of "uniqueness" to a priest's relationship with those he serves. I'm not sure how to describe it but it seems tied up with the particular Christian service that the priest is trying to provide. There's a kind of priority to a priest's mission that dictates the kind of relationships he has with those he serves. Maybe one way of stating the uniqueness of the relationship would be to say that a priest is primarily to serve those people he ministers to rather than enjoy their presence. This is not to say that he can't enjoy the company of those he

serves. It's a question of priority, a matter of
mission. Service seems to dictate the kind of presence and relationship. The priest is not relating
so that he can gain friends but rather so that he
can minister to people. The priest is one who has
"promises to keep" and "miles to go before he
sleeps."

I'm not opting for a priest to play a role or wear
a mask in his ministry. He should be himself and
the more he integrates "servant" with his personality the more real he will be as a minister. Role-
playing in the priestly ministry can be disastrous.

Most priests will remember from their seminary
days sermons on loneliness. Spiritual directors
often warned about the great danger of loneliness
in the priesthood. As I recall, I believed they were
right though I don't think I really understood
what was being said. Now I can strongly affirm the
warning. Loneliness is the feeling of not counting, of not mattering, of not being significant.
Loneliness has no essential connection with the
physical presence or absence of people. You
can be lonely in a crowd and yet when you are
alone not experience loneliness at all. Part of the
difficulty of priestly ministry is the call to profound
personal presence with no strings attached. The
priest's presence to those he serves requires a
faithfulness not just to the individuals he likes or
who like him but to a broader community.

I experience priestly existence as a dialogue
between loneliness and loving. However, the more
I reflect on my experience the more I realize that
all human living is a dialogue between loneliness
and loving. Although in a priest's life the dialogue may assume unique and dramatic shapes, all
persons walk the tightrope between loneliness and
loving. In order to serve the lonely, a priest
needs friends. So does everyone.

The Friendship of Jesus

If we wish to see the incarnation of the ideals of friendship we can look at Jesus. He fulfilled the ideals of friendship in his relationship with his followers. Throughout the Gospel stories, Jesus is offering his friendship to those who will accept him as a friend. He seems unafraid of being hurt or being rejected. What he is about is worth the risk. In the sense that he is always ready to enter into relationship, Jesus made himself quite vulnerable. Even the briefest reflection on our experience reminds us how difficult it is to be vulnerable. Before we offer our friendship to anyone we want a guarantee that we won't get hurt. We are cautious, perhaps overcautious, about entering relationships and about the depth of the relationships we have.

The portrait painted of Jesus in the Gospels suggests Jesus was in no way stingy with his gift of self. He seemed to be about his Father's business and that task colored everything. Because he was calling others to deeper love relationships it was particularly fitting that he allowed himself to be vulnerable. Of course, the classic example of vulnerability is provided by Jesus' relationship with Judas. The missed opportunity of Judas is the great tragedy of history. In turning against Jesus, Judas was committing a kind of suicide, a kind of killing of what was best in himself, which prefigured his physical suicide.

In our description of friendship we have stressed both the healing and creative aspects of friendship. Jesus was known as a healer.

At least as important as the physical healing which Jesus performs is the healing presence which he provides to people. When he is with someone he is really "for that person." His concern and interest seem to come across. This may explain to some extent his tremendous appeal to the apostles.

A friend is someone whose very presence can heal us and help us grow. Jesus seems to have been that kind of presence to people. The physical healings were marvelous, but the personal or spiritual healings may have been more marvelous.

A friend creates us in a way analogous to the way God creates. Of course, a friend does not create us from nothing as God does but it may be that a friend in creating us comes as close to being like God as a human person can. By offering his or her personal presence as a gift, a friend invites us to grow to a new self-identity, a new self-possession. Jesus seems to have done that to each person he met. The Gospel stories are filled with incidents in which Jesus calls a person to a new self-identity. Frequently, Jesus calls a person to a conversion, a genuine and profound change of direction.

Creative Calling

Jesus' presence to people was a marvelous combination of calling them to a new way of loving and yet accepting them as they were. Not many people are good at this but it seems to be essential to true loving. The loving person accepts his or her friend and yet wishes that the friend will continue to grow as a person. Often in our friendship we slip into one extreme or another; either we put conditions on our loving and will not love unless the person agrees to change or we so accept the person that we in no way encourage him or her to grow. Jesus struck the proper balance. He put no conditions on his loving yet he was always calling people beyond themselves.

Probably the characteristic of friendship that most typifies Jesus' relationship with people is the aspect of gift. Friendship really can't be earned or won. It is given freely. This is one of the really beautiful qualities of friendship, that is, it is always a gift. No one has to be my friend. Those who

are have chosen to be friends. Jesus gave his gift
of self freely. The image we get from the Gospels
is of a man who is available. Though he was available there seems to have been no superficiality in
Jesus' presence. He wasn't trying to maneuver
people into relationship or trick people into
friendship.

Vulnerability, healing, acceptance, creativity and
gift are five qualities of friendship that we have
discussed. As with all the attractive aspects of
human nature, the five qualities seem to be exem-
plified in Jesus and in his manner of relating.

CHAPTER FIVE

Loneliness and Jesus

There is a whole generation of Christians — I am among them — who tend to emphasize the divinity of Jesus at the expense of his humanity. Half consciously we so misinterpret everything Jesus did that his actions in the Gospels become a sort of playacting. When we read that he asked questions, we mentally note that because he was God he already knew the answers; when we read that he wept over Lazarus' tomb, we remind ourselves that as God he was infinitely happy. If we follow this tendency to minimize Jesus' humanity too far, we are led to say that he did not really suffer on Calvary. Of course, this is heresy. Jesus really wept; Jesus really suffered; Jesus really died.

If we take seriously the judgment of many scripture scholars that the human consciousness of Jesus grew in awareness of his divinity and perhaps did not reach full awareness until the resurrection, then it seems legitimate to conclude that Jesus experienced all human feelings, including the feeling of loneliness; Jesus at times must have *felt* terribly alone.

The Gospels are infinitely rich. When we read them with faith, we often receive new insights. Even though the word loneliness never appears in the Gospels, it is illuminating to read the Gospels looking for Jesus' attempts to heal loneliness. Such a reading sheds an enormous amount of light on loneliness. Jesus must have been very sensitive to others' loneliness because he was always calling people to a new sense of their importance. He spends his public ministry trying to reveal his Father to people, trying to show them that they are not alone, but that they are passionately loved by his Father. Almost any Gospel scene could be interpreted in terms of Jesus combatting people's loneliness. We will look at just two scenes.

The first scene in Luke, chapter seven, concerns the widow of Naim. When Jesus saw the weeping widow whose only son had died, he must have been deeply moved. Luke reports, "When the Lord saw her he felt sorry for her" (v. 13). Even a less sensitive person than Jesus would have been deeply touched. A mother pours out her love on her son throughout her life. Nothing is too good for her son. What must it be like for a widow to lose her only son? The pain of sorrow, the feelings of lone-liness must be devastating. Sensitive to suffering, Jesus must have felt deeply for her. Luke reports, " 'Do not cry,' he said. Then he went up and put his hand on the bier and the bearers stood still, and he said, 'Young man, I tell you to get up.' And the dead man sat up and began to talk, and Jesus gave him to his mother" (vv. 13-16).

Through the miracle Jesus is indirectly revealing to the widow that she is never completely alone. In the darkest moments, the presence and power of God can help us not only survive but find a deeper meaning and hope.

Another moving Gospel scene involves the sick man at the pool of Bethzatha in the opening verses of chapter five of St. John's Gospel. Once again we have a very human and touching situation. The man had been sick for 38 years. Apparently he had spent much time at the pool hoping to be healed. When Jesus asked him if he wanted to be healed, the man replied, "I have no one to put me in the pool when the water is disturbed, and while I am still on the way, someone else gets there before me" (v. 7). The man must have had severe feelings of loneliness. No one sufficiently cared about him to help him to the pool. Looking at the sick man lying on his mat and seeing the man was so alone that no one would even help him to the pool, Jesus must have been deeply moved. Saying, "Get up, pick up your sleeping-mat and walk" (v. 9), Jesus healed the man's physical infirmity and showed him that someone cared.

These are just two miracles that can serve as examples in the Gospels of Jesus' sensitivity to others' feelings.

Even more than the experience of interpersonal love between people, the most powerful reality either to abolish loneliness or to put it in perspective is the Father's love for us. This was Jesus' basic message: our heavenly Father loves us and wants us to share his kingdom with us. Almost any scene in the Gospel could be interpreted in relation to loneliness because in almost every scene Jesus is trying to help people both to see who they are and to believe in the Father's love for them. Every Christian has favorite texts that speak of the Father's love. One of my favorites is in the sixth chapter of St. Matthew. Jesus, in trying to tell people to trust in his Father, is reported as saying, "That is why I am telling you not to worry about your life and what you are to eat, nor about your body and how you are to clothe it. Surely life means more than food, and the body more than clothing! Look at the birds in the sky. They do not

sow or reap or gather into barns; yet your heavenly Father feeds them. Are you not worth much
more than they are?" (vv. 25-26). Jesus has given
us a marvelous image of the Father's love and concern for us. If we believe Jesus, we can judge that
loneliness never means we are alone or abandoned
in the universe.

However, it is not merely Jesus' miracles or
words that shed light on the meaning of loneliness. His own experience of loneliness and especially his death and resurrection can illuminate the
meaning of loneliness for us.

Perhaps the most lonely moment in history was
Jesus' experience in the Garden of Gethsemane
just before his arrest. Remembering that Jesus
had normal human feelings, we should try to
imagine as vividly as we can what Jesus' experience
in Gethsemane was.

Jesus had been publicly preaching and healing
for three years. He was the most giving kind of
person. Apparently, at least to some people, his
personality was extremely attractive. His small band
of followers seemed to have great loyalty to him.
Though they often missed the point and, at least
prior to Pentecost, did not seem to grasp fully what
Jesus was about, they did evidence some sense of
the importance of Jesus' mission by leaving behind
their previous way of living in order to follow
Jesus.

While the misunderstanding and hardness of
heart that Jesus encountered with some of the
people must have hurt someone who very much
wanted to communicate, the fact that one of his
friends should betray him must have been a horrible blow to Jesus. The handful of apostles were
special to Jesus. To them he had given special
preparation. To have one of the chosen not only
not accept his friendship but hand him over to be
killed must have been very disillusioning for Jesus.

In times of pain and worry, friends can be a tremendous support. It must have been for this reason that Jesus asked Peter, James and John to accompany him to the Garden of Gethsemane. Prayer was the most proper response to the sadness and distress that came over Jesus. Matthew reports, "And sadness came over him, and great distress. Then he said to them, 'My soul is sorrowful to the point of death. Wait here and keep awake with me.' And going on a little further he fell on his face and prayed. 'My Father,' he said, 'if it is possible, let this cup pass me by. Nevertheless, let it be as you, not I, would have it'" (26:37-39).

Three times Jesus returned to his three friends to find them sleeping. They seemed to have had little sense of how much Jesus needed them. The sense of isolation that Jesus experienced must have been enormous. When we really need our friends, ask for their help and then are let down by them, we can experience an intense kind of loneliness. Those upon whom we relied did not come through for us. Jesus must have had an intense experience of loneliness as he prayed in the garden.

Certainly the Gospel writers convey that Jesus was having an intense emotional experience. Whatever the details of that experience were, in spite of any feelings of fear or discouragement or temptations to despair, Jesus delivered himself to his Father. He did not joyfully embrace his sufferings. He wanted them to pass, but he submitted himself to his Father's will.

The entire experience of the passion — the cross-examination, the ridicule, the abandonment by his friends, the beatings, and the crucifixion — must have intensified Jesus' sense of isolation. Yet by lovingly handing himself into his Father's hands, Jesus passes through the loneliness of death into risen life.

Ultimately, for loneliness to be combatted by a Christian, it must be in terms of love of God and being loved by God. All other love merely mirrors God's love; all other love is a drop from the infinite ocean of divine love. Like Jesus, we may be disappointed by our friends; like Jesus, we may find that our gift of love often goes unaccepted. Even in this life our love of God and our realization that God loves us, while it will keep loneliness in perspective, may not completely destroy loneliness. To conceive of the ultimate destruction of loneliness, one must speak of the greatest mystery of Christianity, the mystery of the resurrection.

When Jesus passed through death, he entered into a new way of living that we refer to as risen life. As Christians we believe that all those faithful to God's love will ultimately enter into risen life. Though no one can understand the risen life completely, we can through reflection on the scriptural accounts of the risen Lord and on the Church's teaching gain some notion of what this new life is.

Risen life certainly means the end of all pain and frustration. It seems to mean the most intense kind of love life. This is what Paul tells us in the beautiful 13th chapter of his first letter to the Corinthians. After indicating the superiority of love in relation to other gifts, Paul says, "Love does not come to an end. But if there are gifts of prophecy, the time will come when they must fail; or the gift of tongues, it will not continue for ever; and knowledge — for this, too the time will come when it must fail. For our knowledge is imperfect and our prophesying is imperfect, but once perfection comes, all imperfect things will disappear. . . . Now we are seeing a dim reflection in a mirror, but then we shall be seeing face to face" (vv. 8-10, 12). The intensity of love will lead to a vision of God "face to face." The presence of love that we experience at times in this life as healing and creative will reach its fulfillment in risen life. Whatever person is meant to be will be reached in the resurrection.

It seems safe to say that loneliness will no longer plague us in the risen life. The superficial interpretation of loneliness as a feeling that reveals that a person is not important or loved will have been destroyed along with death by risen life. If loneliness is interpreted as a kind of prophetic feeling, a feeling of being alone that suggests that we ought not to be alone, then the risen life can be looked on as the fulfillment of the promise contained in loneliness. In risen life we will see clearly that we are not meant to be alone but to be united with God and with our brothers and sisters in a community of love. Risen life is love life at its peak.

Chapter Six

Loneliness and Hope

In the mouth of Prince Hamlet, Shakespeare articulated the question that typifies the human struggle:

> To be or not to be — that is the question;
> Whether 'tis nobler in the mind to suffer
> The slings and arrows of outrageous fortune,
> Or to take arms against a sea of troubles,
> And by opposing end them? To die, to sleep —
> No more; and by a sleep to say we end
> The heart-ache and the thousand natural shocks
> That flesh is heir to. 'Tis a consummation
> Devoutly to be wished (Act 3, Scene 1).

The question is right on target: "To be or not to be?" To exist takes a great deal of courage and hope. If given rein, loneliness can crush a person. Suicide is the choice of an increasing number of people. More and more people seem to judge that the "rat race" is just not worth the effort. Many, if they don't commit suicide, engage in various kinds of dropouts and cop-outs that might be described as "emotional or personal

suicides." Many allow their goals to narrow and
shrink and their hope to disappear. This is unfortunate because what is most valuable in a person is
being lost. To be a person is to be a creature of
hope. Loneliness is one of the key experiences
which can reveal this.

To Be Is to Be Dependent

To be a person means to walk a tightrope. No
person is totally in charge of his or her being. Our
being is a received being. I wasn't asked whether
I wanted to exist. I find myself in the world. Occasionally in history, and the 1960's was such a time,
there is a period in which the dignity and great-
ness of being human are glorified. Time and time
again in the 1960's we heard that human beings had
come of age. No matter what accomplishments
are attributed to human persons, their basic de-
pendence must be affirmed: Our being is given to
us, and death seems to take it away.

We become very aware of our fragility when
some serious decision must be made, for example,
a vocational decision, or when a loved one dies,
or when some other tragedy occurs. At such moments we become aware that we are not our own,
that we don't completely control our lives. Because of this, to exist as a person takes hope. A
person must be ready to take risks, to allow the
possibility of failure, to choose values that may not
be easily reached. "Playing it safe" all the time is
ultimately self-defeating for the person. Built into
the nature of a person is the drive to go beyond
what can be clearly proven.

Even friendship involves a self-gift. To play it
safe always, to refuse to take risks, to be overly
cautious, can lead ultimately to an increase of loneliness. Only by leaving the firm ground of the
certain and the evident and walking on the waters
of new discovery in interpersonal relationships can
a person overcome loneliness. Sometimes this

venturing into new relationships can be relatively easy; at times it is quite difficult. It always takes some courage. Occasionally the lonely person may need heroic courage.

Such courage is not easily manufactured. Some think that courage is its own reward. For example, some existentialists and writers connected with the theater of the absurd seem to be saying that life has no meaning and that the courageous struggle for survival is its own reward. The position makes little sense. It is as absurd as the universe to which it responds. For courage to make any kind of sense, it has to be rooted in some meaningful universe. The meaning of reality, or perhaps it would be better to say the mystery of reality, need not be clear, but for courage to have value there must be some hope. If courage is its own and only reward, then we are like mere animals trying to die with some dignity.

Camus' Challenge

One of the most eloquent and sensitive spokesmen for the dignity of persons in an absurd world was atheist Albert Camus. The ending of his powerful novel, *The Plague*, is a beautiful piece of writing, a touching hymn to the dignity of persons in a meaningless world. The plague having ended, Camus' hero, Dr. Rieux, ends his chronicle by pointing out that though the townsfolk are rejoicing the plague would return to challenge persons to transcend their mediocrity.

> None the less, he knew that the tale he had to tell could not be one of final victory. It could be only the record of what had had to be done, and what assuredly would have to be done again in the never-ending fight against terror and its relentless onslaughts, despite their personal afflictions, by all who, while unable to be

saints but refusing to bow down to pestilences, strive their utmost to be healers.

And, indeed, as he listened to the cries of joy rising from the town, Rieux remembered that such joy is always imperilled. He knew what those jubilant crowds did not know but could have learned from books: that the plague bacillus never dies or disappears for good; that it can be dormant for years and years in furniture and linen-closets; that it bides its time in bedrooms, cellars, trunks, and bookshelves; and that perhaps the day would come when, for the bane and the enlightenment of men, it would rouse up its rats again and send them forth to die in a happy city.[1]

Though this piece of writing is a wonderful plea for personal responsibility, Camus did not push his insight into the beauty of person sufficiently far. Unless there is hope for a "final victory," unless there is hope against death in all its forms, persons cannot have dignity, but are reduced to absurd dreamers engaged in self-deception. Unless there is hope for a final victory against death, loneliness wins: persons are hopelessly alone. For courage to make any sense, a person must be able to hope against all death experiences. Hope helps us to move creatively into the future.

In Samuel Becket's play, *Waiting for Godot,* one of the classics of the theater of the absurd and a frightening depiction of man's experience of lack of meaning and purpose, the two main characters often talk about motion. They are waiting for some mysterious character named Godot with whom they have an appointment. They wonder if they should wait for him or move on to some other place. Though there is much talk of motion there is no significant or meaningful motion. The characters seem to move around in circles. No one has

---

[1]*The Plague,* Albert Camus, trans. by Stuart Gilbert, © 1972, Random House, Inc.

any real destination. Both acts of the play end
similarly. One character suggests that they should
move on and the other character agrees. However, as the lights dim neither character moves.
Loneliness can make our lives seem as directionless
as the two characters in the play; it can lock us in
a corner.

No Standing Still

There is an axiom oft-quoted by retreat masters
and spiritual directors that since the spiritual life
is a life, you must either be progressing or
losing ground. There is no standing still. In the
axiom there is a profound truth related to the
meaning of Christian hope. There is only one way
to approach the Christian life and that is whole-
heartedly. To intend to live the Christian life in
some lesser way is to intend to follow some way
other than that offered through Christ.

There is a sense in which hope is distinctive-
ly human. No other creature in our experience
hopes. Animals can be instinctively expectant. For
example, a dog can associate a particular footstep
with a series of pleasing experiences and memories that add up to his "master." But human hope
is intellectual. It is connected with a vision of what
might be possible for man. Human hope sees new
possibilities for humanity. Christian hope sees
possibilities for man beyond man's wildest dreams.

Thirteen years ago my sister died suddenly at
the age of 36. Within the 10-year period following,
my mother lost two sisters, a brother and my father.
Except for me, my mother has no living immediate
family. Though she doesn't easily talk about her
loved ones who have died, my mother, who is
very active, told me that at night if she can't sleep, all
sorts of memories flood her consciousness. Without planning to, and probably without wanting to,
she thinks of different incidents with her family.
The way she describes these thoughts is, "They

come to me while I'm lying there unable to sleep."
Activity during the day keeps her mind busy but
at night the memories take over. I know the experience. It's analogous to worry or anxiety.
Though you don't want to worry, the unconscious
thoughts won't be banished. My mother also told
me that every night without exception she dreams
of one or more of her loved ones who have died.
What can be kept at the corner of unconsciousness
during the working hours rules during sleep. Starting with my sister's death 13 years ago, my mother's
life has been a battle with loneliness, a battle that
has taken enormous courage and hope. My
mother's Christian hope denies that death is the
end of persons.

Rooted in Reality

Reflection on hope reveals that the virtue of
hope is always centered on another person. We
don't really hope in something, we always hope in
someone. In a very provocative essay, "The Virtue
of Hope" in his book, *Building the Human,* Robert
Johann makes clear the difference between the
virtue of hope and both naive optimism and the
natural desires that everyone has. The virtue of
hope is both more realistic and more demanding
than the latter two.

All of us know Pollyanna people who are naive-
ly optimistic. For them everything is always wonderful. They seem incapable of admitting that
life might be better at least in some areas than it
is now. Somehow to admit difficulties is not possible for them. I once heard of a teacher whom
this description fit. On a morning in which there
were horrendous rainstorms, he entered a classroom and said, "Isn't it a beautiful day!" As the class
gasped he added, "In a wet sort of way." Such
naive optimism is totally unrealistic: it refuses to face
the difficulties and disappointments that enter
every life. Virtues must always be rooted in the

real, and this is no less true of hope than it is of love.

Nor is hope identical with the normal everyday desires that every person has, though the word "hope" is often used to express those desires: "I hope it doesn't rain," "I hope I get a raise," "I hope I meet some nice people." To have such desires is quite normal and really does not require any virtue. Only through hope can a person develop. Only through hope can loneliness be overcome. Only through hope can love happen.

As we said in Chapter Three, only loving and being loved can conquer loneliness or at least put it into perspective. Love can't happen without hope. When I put myself at the service of someone, when I offer myself as a gift to someone, when in effect I say, "I am for you," there is no way I can guarantee that the beloved will accept me. Every act of loving is risky. It requires hope. If I don't hope that the other will respond, then I can't love, and if I don't love, then I will be crushed by loneliness. When I love, I hope in the other. I am hoping that my gift will be received and accepted. In a sense, within every act of love is the request, "Let me love you" or "Please accept my love" or "I hope you will accept my love." One reason why the lover hopes is that the lover realizes that he or she can't be a person without loving. Personal development depends on an individual's capacity to love. Because hope is a necessary ingredient in loving, hope is as essential for personal growth as love is.

Hope Is a Risk

Of course, we can learn through experience that certain people are not reliable. Prudence tells us not to count on them. All hope involves a risk, but the *one* other upon whom we can hope recklessly is our heavenly Father. Just as hope is essential for growth in human relationships, it is essential for

growth in relationships between God and human
persons. Ultimately it is only hope in God and
love of God which will deliver us from loneliness.
All other loves, as beautiful as they are, receive
their power from God's love and without his
presence would lose their capacity to heal. The
human heart is so constructed that only God can
fill it.

In the book of Revelation a wonderful line is
attributed to God by the author: "I know all about
you; and now I have opened in front of you a
door that nobody will be able to close. . ." (3:8).
The image is marvelous. Life can be looked at
in terms of the metaphor of open doors. Each
new possibility, each chance at growth, is an open
door. Family, friends, studies, theater, party, film,
places and circumstances are opportunities for
doors to open. The love given by one human being
to another can open a new door that for most
people is the most important door. Possibilities
that were only dreams become actualized. Human
existence takes on new dimensions and depths. To
the person who is loved, being human has a more
profound and important meaning than it had before love was experienced.

Yet within human experience doors are constantly being closed. Possibilities are excluded to
the sick and poor and lonely. Opportunities are
missed. Many apparent chances for growth are not
what they first appear. Dreams are crushed, ave-
nues narrowed. Yet God says he has opened a
door which no one will be able to close. It is
God's door upon which our hope is based. Because
of the Incarnation there are possibilities for men
of which man would not even have dreamed.
God's word has transformed humanity's capacities
for love. What encourages and strengthens hope
is that no one can shut God's door — no person,
no power, no force, no evil can close the door God
has opened for men.

We can hope because the God who is revealed in salvation history is a God who keeps his promises. He is a God who is always calling us into the future, asking us to leave what is secure and safe and to launch out into the unknown. What enables us to do that is God's love for us and his promise to us. Our God is a God of promise and a God who keeps his promises. He kept his promises to Abraham, to Moses, to the chosen people. Most importantly, he kept his promise concerning Jesus.

Not a Cheap Grace

To hope in God is to place yourself in his hands, to trust in his presence. This does *not* mean that every problem in your life will work out exactly the way you plan. To think this would be to equate love with desire. On the occasion of a death of a loved one, it can become clear that those mourning have misunderstood hope. They will say something like, "My parents were so good. They never did anything wrong. Why did God let them die?" The mourners have put restrictions on God's love that can't be found in Christian revelation. When or where did God reveal that those who loved him and kept his commandments would not suffer and die? The large number of people who react to tragedy as though God has gone back on his word reveals that there is widespread misunderstanding by many religious people. To hope in God is to trust that ultimately his love will take care of us. To hope in God is to give him infinite credit. There is a sense in which hope always says, "in spite of everything." Hope is a way of seeing beyond the "evidence" that tells us that we should not hope.

False Hopes and Loneliness

Unreal expectations concerning interpersonal relationships within the human community can intensify rather than heal loneliness. If persons think of love relationships in images of handholding and walking into the sunset, then they are bound to be let down. Their expectations are unreal. Love is the greatest human experience and it does put all other realities into perspective, but it does not remove suffering, tragedy and death from human existence. To dream that it does or to refuse to face the existence of suffering is to refuse to face reality. To allow unreal expectations is to court loneliness. When the letdown comes, a person will feel alone and abandoned because reality turned out differently than imagined.

There can also be cultural factors contributing to loneliness. Contemporary theater, film and literature brilliantly depict loneliness. However, if our artists can do no more than portray loneliness in all its sadness, if they offer no saving or redeeming images, then they may be fostering loneliness.

Today, institutions also may greatly contribute to people's loneliness. At least one of the reasons for the campus riots in the 1960's was the strong reaction of the students to being reduced to a number on a file card. The logic behind barricading a dean's office or sitting on a president's desk was that attention must be paid to students. Of course, a person can have unreal expectations of an institution. We should choose carefully which institutions we will allow to form us, but once we have chosen, we shouldn't romanticize them. For example, in the Church it is important that individual priests and sisters be respected and that their talents and wishes concerning assignments be considered seriously. However, either through injustice, which can stain all institutions, or for the best reason in the world, namely, that a group needs someone for a specific service, it may happen that the preferences of the priest or sister may have to take a backseat. To be part of any community is to surrender some of your own preferences and desires. To romanticize institutions is to set yourself up for the plague of loneliness.

Balance Is Important

We have a tendency to fantasize or mythologize the evils in our lives. While doing a little research into the Old Testament I discovered that one of the original reasons why the ancients built walls around their cities was to keep out demons. This fantasizing or mythologizing of evil is a characteristic of the Jewish people evident in the Psalms. For the Jewish people, God was the one through whom evil was demythologized and put into perspective. Because Yahweh was their God, the Jewish people believed that no evil could crush them.

Behind the use of the word "fantasizing" or "mythologizing" is the idea of blowing out of proportion. I find that I am constantly fantasizing and mythologizing the evil in my life. I am in constant battle with myself to keep in proper perspective the evil I experience in myself and in my surroundings. It is easy to become anxious and frightened. Problems loom large and solutions seem beyond reach. Aid is not always available and at times not even foreseeable.

Occasionally, without even being able to cite accurately the cause of the fear, I feel anxious and timorous. I become anxious about future loneliness: Will I be able to handle it? I find others experiencing the same kind of anxiety. My friend, who broke down in tears at a wake, was fantasizing her future loneliness. To keep a balance, to be optimistic, to see clearly the nature, amount and extent of evil in our lives are extremely difficult. We keep fantasizing and mythologizing; our outlook on evil becomes blurred. If we excessively fantasize evil in relation to our pursuit of the Christian life, then the ultimate result may be despair. We may judge that we cannot reach the goal to which God is calling us. We may judge that our own weakness and selfishness put us beyond redemption.

Hope Is Antidote

The proper antidote to our tendency to fantasize evil is the virtue of hope. I am not suggesting that we be naive. To be a Pollyanna is not a virtue. Hope gives us a realistic perspective on our lives; it keeps facts in some kind of order. More importantly, it keeps us aware of the most important facts. It keeps us moored to the ground upon which the kingdom of God is built. Hope keeps us rooted in the Resurrection and enables us to see all evils in that perspective. To trust in the risen Lord is not to solve all problems, but without the risen Lord no problem is ultimately solvable.

One of my favorite poems is Peter Viereck's "Game Called on Account of Darkness."[1] Though I first read it more than 20 years ago I find that the poem has a lasting significance for me. Viereck's poetic depiction of a man who has lost his faith is sufficiently rooted in human experience so that it can speak to any adult. Comparing life to a game, Viereck points out that when he was a child the rules of the game were clear because he had a friend who watched him from the sky and gave him the rules of the game. Now that he is a man the friend is no longer present. The rules of the game of life are no longer clear and a nostalgia is experienced:

> Once there was a friend
> He watched me from the sky.
> Maybe he never lived at all.
> Maybe too much friendship made him die.
>
> When the gang played cops and robbers in
>   the alley.
> It was my friend who told me which were which.
> Now he doesn't tell me any more.
> (Which team am I playing for?)

---

[1] From the Pulitzer prize-winning book of poems, *Terror & Decorum,* available from Greenwood Press, Westport, CN, 1972, © by Peter Viereck.

He was like a kind of central-heating
In the big cold house, and that was good.
One by one I have to chop my toys now,
As firewood.

Every time I stood upon a crossroads,
It made me mad to feel him watch me choose.
I'm glad there's no more spying while I play
Still I'm sad he went away.

There is a danger today that people will experience a nostalgia for God. We can allow God's in-
volvement in our lives to become merely a memory
like Latin Masses or novenas or the enthusiasm gen-
erated among people during John F. Kennedy's
presidency. We believe that God is never a memory. God is better characterized, as some contemporary process thinkers describe him, as the never-
to-be-caught-up-with-future. God is alive and in
front of us. In a period when much that we
thought was firmly moored down has become un-
stuck, we have to remind ourselves that God is
always more than any of our images of him. While
certain forms of religion and worship may be tied
to the past, God is never tied to the past. Even the
past events of salvation history have a future
orientation to them. God acted among the Jewish
people to lead them into the future, to lead them
into a deeper relationship with him. There is a
sense in which every salvation event is a call and a
promise. Each event is God's invitation to enter
more deeply into his friendship. Even Jesus'
Resurrection is a call to us. The risen Lord is before
us, opening new possibilities of life and love for
us. If we trust in him the God of the future will
not allow loneliness to drown us.

God Not a Bystander

There is a religious devotion encouraged by
spiritual writers which is often referred to as "prac-

ticing the presence of God." One goal of the devotion is an increased awareness of God's involve-
ment in human life. Some belief in God's presence
is essential if salvation is to have any relevant
meaning. God is neither a memory nor a disinterested bystander. Wherever we are, whatever
difficulty we are experiencing, whatever suffering
is ours, whatever evil threatens us, whatever abandonment and loneliness we feel, we are able to
hope. If we hope, no evil is so ominous that it can
kill the God who is present, calling us into the
future. The presence of the risen Lord means that
there is no human situation in which God cannot
be found. Hope means God hasn't gone away.
Hope means we are not alone.

For me the classic statement of Christian hope is
a section from St. Paul's letter to the Philippians.
After telling the community at Philippi that he has
received all sorts of advantages because of being a
Hebrew, the Apostle stresses that in comparison
with commitment to Christ previous advantages
can be looked upon as disadvantages.

Not only that, but I believe that nothing can
happen that will outweigh the supreme advantage of knowing Christ Jesus my Lord. For him
I have accepted the loss of everything as so
much rubbish if only I can have Christ and be
given a place in him. I am no longer trying for
perfection that comes from the Law, but I want
only the perfection that comes through faith
in Christ, and is from God and based on faith.
All I want is to know Christ and the power of
his resurrection and to share his sufferings by
reproducing the pattern of his death. That is
the way I can hope to take my place in the
resurrection of the dead. Not that I have become perfect yet: I have not yet won, but I am
still running, trying to capture the prize for
which Christ Jesus captured me. I can assure

you, my brothers, I am far from thinking that I have already won. All I can say is that I forget the past and I strain ahead for what is still to come. I am racing for the finish, for the prize to which God calls us upwards in Christ Jesus.

To hope is to change the atmosphere. Hope is infectious. The person who hopes mirrors the God of hope; his hope calls people into the future.

To combat loneliness, our expectations must be real. That does not mean that they must be small. The Christian gives God infinite credit. Like St. Paul, he believes that "the one who began the good work in you will see that it is finished when the day of Christ Jesus comes" (Phil 1:6). To battle loneliness, hope is required. Feelings of loneliness shouldn't discourage us. Those feelings may be calling us to be our best selves.

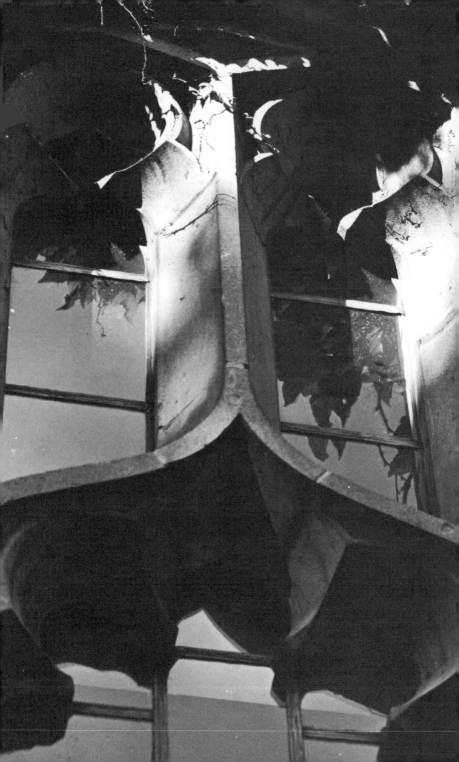

Chapter Seven

Loneliness and Prayer

If loneliness is to be understood and combatted, there must be some understanding of prayer. For the Christian, any serious discussion and analysis of loneliness must include a discussion of prayer because prayer reveals who we are. Ultimately, it is because prayer is possible that we are not alone in some hostile universe.

I suppose prayer always has been and always will be a problem for some of us. It ought to be very easy. Believing that God is present, we ought to turn to him readily and frequently. The experience of many of us, however, is that what we ought to do is not necessarily what we do.

There are probably large numbers who have no serious difficulty with prayer. Either they have sufficiently worked out their prayer problems or they are among that special group who never had difficulty with prayer. Probably any sketching of present problems that people are experiencing in prayer will seem strange and foreign to those whose prayer life proceeds with little disturbance.

A Recent Phenomenon

Within the last 10 or 15 years a significant number of Christians have questioned and changed their prayer practices. One of the more obvious examples is afforded by the change that has occurred in houses of religious. Where formerly prayer schedules and prayer formulations went unquestioned for years and years, striking changes have taken place. Either prayer schedules have disappeared completely or have been minimized. Today a visit to a novitiate or seminary chapel might mean witnessing a mass media presentation rather than a group reciting the rosary.

This does not mean that in religious communities or houses of formation movies have replaced prayer. Nor does it mean that authorities have decided that prayer is not an essential element in the formation of Christian persons. It does mean that serious and radical questions have been and are being asked about the meaning and manner of prayer.

Trying to characterize the past experience of prayer is difficult. The danger is that we will take a "nothing but" approach to previous emphases in prayer. We can slip into the erroneous myopic views expressed in the following statements: "In the past prayer was nothing but routine and mechanical recitation," or "We used to emphasize 'nothing but' the quantity of prayer and the time spent in prayer but now we are stressing the quality of prayer." Both of these expressions are ridiculous in their one-sidedness. Man has been genuinely praying since he recognized himself as man. Christians have been offering authentic prayer since Jesus' Resurrection.

At any time prayer is as conditioned as the rest of Christian life. God is always present to man but man's turning to God is influenced by all the cultural and historical factors to which man is heir.

Both man's self-understanding and his understanding of prayer are influenced by the time in history
during which man exists. Although Christianity
does contain God's truth, how much of that truth
filters to an individual Christian depends on many
factors.

In looking back at the past we can think that our
present position, merely because it is present, is
privileged. Probably just as we can look back at
an off-center emphasis concerning prayer, people
in the future will find it easy to articulate dimensions of prayer that we are missing. In trying to
capture what changed in the consciousness of
many Christians I am afraid that any descriptions
of mine will be an oversimplification.

One way to characterize our previous understanding and emphases in prayer is to say that a
monastic approach and emphasis were judged
suitable for everyone. In the minds of many of us
the number of prayers and the amount of time
spent in prayer each day received too much weight.
Set formulas were emphasized more than prayer
from the heart. We felt guilty when we neglected
prayer even when the substituted action was an
act of charity. When a sufficiently large number
saw the problems that this understanding and emphasis in prayer were creating, changes began
to occur. Of course, the danger of "throwing out
the baby with the bathwater" is ever-present. This
seemed to happen to some during the "secular
sixties." There is a danger that once we realize
that other activities besides prayer are important,
we quickly infer that every human action is a
prayer. Such a view can mean that no real prayer
is said. I can never remember a time in my life
when so many people were looking for a meaning
that can only be discovered in prayer.

Change in Consciousness

While prayer is an art that many of us will always be learning rather than having achieved, recent history has been a time of particular crisis. My own opinion is that what has caused the crisis in prayer is a change in consciousness. Because we think of ourselves differently today, much of what we did unquestioningly in the past we feel we can no longer do. We think, for example, that the genuinely important area of life is "action" and that thought or prayer is a luxury for those who are less zealous and less apostolic. What counts is to "do something," not to engage in actionless reflection.

Looking back on my four years as a curate in a parish, I feel that one of the more important parish experiences was moderating discussion clubs. Yet it was an activity that constantly needed justification whenever I discussed experiences with classmates. The ever-present implied indictment was that discussion was relatively useless and that detailed external activity should always be preferred. The experience of discussion groups, however, continually destroyed the myth. Through discussion people changed, through discussion new understandings of God were born; fresh insights into life were nurtured and new self-images emerged. Far from being unimportant, a change in consciousness may be the most dramatic event.

The crisis in prayer has come about because of a significant change in consciousness. Man has a new self-image in which his freedom and autonomy are emphasized and he has a new image of religion. These new images put strain on previous understandings and emphases concerning prayer and prayer practices. The crisis in prayer was particularly obvious during what I have called the "secular sixties."

"Honest to God"

The shift that took place in man's self-understanding and in his understanding of religion was
clearly and provocatively described by John A. T.
Robinson, then Anglican Bishop of Woolwich, in
his bestselling book, *Honest to God,* published in
1963. That the small paperback book should have
been so popular is in itself significant. Though the
topics he discussed — Christian doctrine, meaning
of God, prayer, sacraments — are not topics
which usually lead to large sales, the ex-bishop's
treatment of these subjects obviously struck the
chords of interest among large audiences. People
were experiencing problems and Robinson seemed
to articulate the problems accurately and speak to
them meaningfully. Robinson's chapter on prayer
is a pretty good summary of what seemed to be
at the root of what happened to many in the 1960's.

Trying to describe an old notion of the "religious," Robinson pointed out that a basic understanding of it was that it was the opposite of the
"secular." The religious or "supernatural" was
contrasted with the world. In describing the religious sphere in the past, many limited it to what
went on in sacred areas or at least limited it to
sacred activities as distinct from secular or worldly
activities. Robinson correctly pointed out that this
understanding would tend to limit prayer to "religion" rather than to "life." Prayer can become
identified with the holy rather than the common,
with the special rather than the everyday, with the
heavenly rather than the worldly.

In trying to stress the error that this too-narrow
conception of prayer contains, Robinson pointed
out how Holy Communion seems to involve Christians in a much broader conception of prayer:

> And yet the sacrament which forms the heart of
> Christian worship is the standing denial of all
> this. It is the assertion of the "beyond" *in*

the midst of life, the holy *in* the common. The
Holy Communion is *the* point at which the
common, the communal, becomes the carrier of
the unconditioned, as the Christ makes himself known in the breaking and sharing of
bread. Holy Communion is communion, com-
munity-life, in *sacris,* in depth, at the level at
which we are not merely in human fellowship
but "in Christ" — not merely in love but in
Love, united with the ground and restorer of
our whole being. At least that is what Communion should be. But too often it is not the
place at which the common and the communal
point through to the beyond in their midst, to
the transcendent in, with and under them, but
precisely the opposite. It ceases to be the holy
meal, and becomes a religious service in which
we turn our backs on the common and the
community and in individualistic devotion
"make our communion" with "God out there."[1]

To stress his point Robinson calls attention to
the significance of something as simple as the position of the minister during worship. The priest
standing with his back to the people can have the
psychological effect of focusing attention somewhere beyond the sanctuary. The suggestion that
we find God by turning from the world, by leaving
the world, can be strengthened. By contrast, the
minister facing the people can suggest that God is
present among them, indeed in their very gathering
together. Robinson stresses that liturgy should not
simply create another world of its own, a world
which simply goes on side by side with real life.

Private prayer is not exempted from this dualistic
stress and emphasis. Robinson pointed out that
private prayer can be conceived in terms of turning
aside from the business of the world in order to
be with God. A strong assumption is that the heart

---

[1]From *Honest To God,* by John A. T. Robinson. The
Westminster Press. © SCM Press Ltd. 1963. Used by permission.

of prayer is withdrawal. That prayer is not with-drawal, however, is one of the reasons why it is such a powerful force against loneliness.

No Positive Vision

Robinson's remarks typify a shift in conscious-ness that occurred in many people in the 60's. There was a reaction against a too-narrow under-standing of prayer. Yet something was lost in the 60's. Though we killed a too-narrow understand-ing of prayer, we did not come up with an under-standing that was able to sustain us. Seeing that prayer was not limited to set formulas or set time periods, we half-consciously bought the position that every human activity was prayer. Though it is a generalization, I think it is true to say that large numbers experienced an impoverishment of spirit. Something got lost, something was missing.

The 70's are telling a different story. Every-where, both within and outside the Christian com-munity, there is a search for something more, for deeper roots, for more enriching experiences. The secular has let us down. Man is looking elsewhere or at least looking for a different meaning to life and the world. The crisis concerning prayer that many of us have gone through or are going through may be a marvelous opportunity for growth. The questions we have concerning prayer may lead to answers which don't come merely from ourselves.

The secular 60's are over; many are disillusioned and a new quest for prayer seems to have arisen. From hippies to drug cultists, from mysticism to devil worship, there is a desire for what is more than human. We may someday characterize this decade as the "searching 70's." The search for meaning has been intensified, and you can't ask many real questions about life or about loneliness without raising questions about prayer.

Though many of us have heard definitions and descriptions of prayer since we began studying catechism, another look at prayer, a slightly different analysis, may lead to an understanding of prayer and a vision of prayer that can revitalize and renew our prayer experience.

New Understanding

For a working definition of prayer I am going to borrow the one offered by Gregory Baum in his book, *Man Becoming*. Baum points out that the traditional definition of prayer as the elevation of the mind and heart to God is inadequate and misleading. This definition neglects that which makes prayer possible, that without which no prayer can take place, namely, the initiative of God. What is essential, if prayer is to take place and if prayer is going to be understood as an activity that can change our lives and put loneliness into proper perspective, is that God speaks first. It is only because of God's speech, God's call and summons, only because of God's invitation that man can speak.

Gregory Baum defines prayer as listening and responding to the divine word. I like this definition for two reasons. First, there can be included within it every activity that I know of that can legitimately be called prayer, and secondly because reflection on the definition can expand and intensify our understanding of prayer, life and loneliness.

Using Baum's definition of prayer, then, I offer my own reflections on that definition with the hope of clarifying the meaning of prayer and of shedding light on prayer's power in relation to the experience of loneliness.

What has to be stressed is that God has spoken his Word, Jesus, to all men. This word is present to us in the Gospel, in the sacraments, in the liturgy and in both the formal and informal recitation of words directed to God. Because of Jesus' Resurrection, however, the word is not limited to these more obviously sacred or holy areas of human life. Because through his Resurrection Jesus is no longer limited by time and space, the Word is present and available in all areas of human living. God speaks to man everywhere and always. Wherever and whenever man listens and responds to God's word, prayer happens.

Prayer is always personal. There have to be genuine or real listening and responding, or prayer does not take place. Merely apparent listening and responding do not suffice. Perhaps an example will make this point clear. When the Gospel is proclaimed at the Eucharist, this is a situation in which prayer ought to take place. But prayer does not happen unless real listening and responding take place. By listening I mean more than sounds resounding in an ear. I mean *someone* is open and concerned about God's message, interested and ready to act on that message. To be physically within hearing distance of the voice of the proclaimer is not necessarily to be a listening presence before God's word.

Real listening is personal. It means not that my ear receives sound waves but that I am receptive and attentive to the speaker and to his message. The lack of real listening during a liturgy may explain to some extent why we are not challenged and transformed through the proclamation of God's word. Perhaps very little prayer is happening.

Prayer Everywhere

While we expect prayer to happen at a liturgical service, we can forget that it can happen whenever and wherever man is listening and responding to God's word. Because God's word is available to man in the ordinary circumstances of day-to-day living, prayer can happen anywhere. A man, if he is listening and responding to God's word while reading the daily newspaper, is praying. In the account of world events and daily news, God's word is present.

I think this example of a newspaper is a good one and I'd like to emphasize it. A number of years ago I heard the brilliant lay theologian, Frank Sheed, discussing the Catholic novelist, Graham Greene. Sheed indicated that what made the highly esteemed British novelist a Catholic novelist was that he made religion extremely real and concrete. According to Sheed, Graham Greene wrote as though the headline on the morning paper was "Son of God Died on a Cross."

My point is this: If we understand the meaning of prayer, then there is a sense in which the headline on every daily paper is "Son of God Died on a Cross." Every newspaper can be read under the light of God's word to man.

By reflecting on the meaning of prayer all our human activities can attain a new importance. They are potentially prayer experiences. To listen and respond to God's word is man's vocation. This is another way of saying, to be human is to pray. The meaning of prayer shows that we need never be alone. Life is a dialogue between God and us.

An atheist, even while remaining an atheist, can pray. Though this seems a strange statement I think it is true. God's word is present in human life. Prayer is listening and responding to the word of God. If the atheist is genuinely listening and responding to God's word in some situation, then that activity is praying. If the atheist is open to what he thinks is right, if he is, for example, in good conscience trying to detect what is morally the right action to perform, then he may be praying.

Admittedly the example of the atheist is an extreme example. I use it because its very extremeness can help us to see that all of life is an opportunity for prayer. This is one of the aspects of Christianity that is particularly marvelous. Every aspect of life can be holy. All of life can be a dialogue which strengthens our awareness that we are not alone because God is with us.

Not Every Activity Is Prayer

Aware that the example of the atheist can be easily misunderstood, I wish to make clear that not every activity is a prayer merely because it is done by man. For an activity to be prayerful, there must be some way in which it can be considered as listening and responding to God's word. If there are genuine listening and responding to what is more than merely human words, I would say it is prayer.

The word of God can come through men or through events and circumstances, but the word is never merely or only a human word or a historical event. If we are genuinely listening, then God's word can be detected through human words and through simple incidents. If we are not really listening, then the presence of God's word may be overlooked.

A final example from my own experience may clarify this. Recently I was bothered by a set of choices that were presented to me. The decision I had to make became more and more a burden to me. In my own mind I gave the decision an importance that outweighed its real importance. I was losing perspective. Tense and nervous, preoccupied with the imminent decision, bothered that I found it so difficult to decide, I experienced signs of anxiety. A tightening in the stomach was accompanied by a restlessness in sleep. Though the decision was important, my anxiety moved me to wish that the choices had never been presented, that I did not have to make the decision.

Finally, I casually told a friend of mine about the two choices open to me. Immediately, with

deep interest, real concern for me and honest enthusiasm for one of the two choices open to me, my friend responded. With touching, moving friendship, with an unfeigned interest in my welfare, the person responded to my need for help and gave advice that was obviously geared toward my best interest.

Almost immediately, even while my friend was still speaking, the anxiety left me. The decision, which formerly had seemed so difficult, became easy. Looking back at that experience, I think that God's word calling me into the future was present in the interest and concern of my friend. The experience with my friend could have been a prayer experience. It is difficult to have certitude about such experiences but looking back on it, this is how I interpret it. My friend's concern freed me so that I could make what I think was the right decision. I believe God was present through my friend.

Admittedly, the example of the atheist or the example from my own life is not what we usually mean when we refer to prayer. I mention them because they can help us to be mindful that not only formal or set periods of reflection are prayer experiences. As we think about the importance of listening and responding to God's word in the daily events of our lives, what becomes obvious is the essential role of set periods of more formal prayer.

Christians Have Advantage
To listen and respond to God's word in ordinary human activities is not easy. It takes courage, attentiveness and faith. It takes perseverance and trust. Christians have a great advantage in trying to listen to God's word in human activities because they are familiar with God's word through the scriptures and the sacraments.

For most Christians it can be expected that

there will be a parallel between their praying in liturgical and private prayer and their praying in the everyday activities of their lives. St. Paul has urged us, "In your minds you must be the same as Christ Jesus" (Phil. 2: 5). We are to put on the mind of Jesus. We are to see things the way Jesus sees them.

Through liturgical prayer and private prayer, through the scriptures and special reading, through homilies and devotions, our mind is opened to the mind of Christ. Our consciousness can be transformed through such activities. It can become sensitized to God's word. When it does become so sensitized, our prayer life will expand. We will be able to discern that the world, rather than being a lonely and hostile place, is charged with the grandeur and glory of God.

In the last few years the word "encounter" has increased in usage. Along with "commitment" and "dialogue" the word is so often used that there is a danger that it will join the ranks of the trite and the cliched. This would be unfortunate. In its most profound meaning, the word can tell us a great deal about loneliness and how to combat it. For me the word captures an element, an aspect, a depth that is present in special meetings between people. "Encounter" can suggest the most intimate and profound kind of meeting. The word can be particularly fruitful in exploring the meaning of prayer.

To highlight how prayer is an encounter between God and man it can be helpful to explore the meaning of encounter in human relationships. The experience of meeting someone can take place on a number of different levels. Three simple examples of persons meeting one another may help to illuminate the meaning of encounter.

A person can meet another briefly and superficially. They are introduced, exchange a few pleasantries — that is the extent of their meeting. No real depth is reached. The way the word "encounter" is used today, it would not apply to such a meeting. Too much is missing from such a meeting to call it an encounter. The meeting has not really done anything to either person. Nothing significant or important has happened.

Another example would be two persons who have not only met but who have come to spend a great deal of time together. They may even know each other for a number of years. However, they feel there is something lacking in their relationship. There is a level they have not reached. In various ways they wear masks, play roles, and assume postures. They do not reveal their true selves.

This kind of relationship is encouraged by our society. We are encouraged to play roles and to wear masks. We are encouraged to "appear" and to "seem" rather than to be.

The word "encounter" should not be used to express the meeting between people who base their relationship on appearances. Their real selves are not involved. In some way, perhaps in various ways, the persons conceal their real selves from one another. Such a relationship is a missed opportunity for growth.

The third example is that of a profound meeting. Two people are genuinely open to each other. They meet each other in such a way that each at the level of his deepest self is present to the other. This type of meeting is what is usually meant today when the word "encounter" is used. The word is an attempt at capturing and expressing something special, something extraordinary. This meeting is "real" in a way the other two I described are not. The meeting takes place on the level of the real self and not on the level of appearances.

Such a meeting may take place between two

people early in their relationship or after years of friendship. While a relationship that has matured over a long period of time is more likely to foster genuine encounters, we know from our experience that a profound meeting can occur between people who have neither known each other a long period nor have spent much time with each other. It seems that some people are more capable of being open to others, more capable of being present to others. Such people seem to have reached a maturity and a freedom which the rest of us lack.

Results of Encounter

What is particularly important in relating human encounter to prayer is to note what human encounters do to people who have them. Persons are special kinds of beings. All living creatures are subject to rules and laws of growth. Plants and animals grow according to certain laws. Persons are also subject to laws if they are to grow. Persons have special needs which must be fulfilled if the persons are going to mature and become more free. If persons are to grow they need other persons. If persons are to conquer loneliness they need other persons.

A genuine encounter, a profound meeting between persons is a special opportunity for personal growth. By meeting together, by being open to another, I have a chance to grow. In a real sense, another person's openness, concern, interest and love create me. The other person helps me to be a person, helps me to grow personally, helps me to have courage, to face life and its difficulties. What is especially important is that the other person's love helps me to love.

If we use the word "encounter" to describe a prayer experience, then we see that all the values that a human encounter has are intensified and surpassed when man encounters God. While my human friends may fail me occasionally, may disappoint me or not be present to me when I especially need them, God is the Other who never fails, disappoints or is absent. God is always present, ready to encounter us. He is always ready to help us grow and mature, to help us be courageous, to help us to be lovers.

In human relationships an encounter is a marvelous experience. Life seems to take on a new value, a new dimension when you encounter another human being. Life intensifies, loneliness recedes. To pray is to encounter God. Praying is a little like breathing. You have to do it if you want to stay alive. It's the thing to do if you want to be a person.

Encounters in Scripture

In the history of salvation as contained in the Old and New Testaments, we have the record of a number of encounters between God and man. All these encounters are mysterious, but they are privileged records through which we can learn about our own relationship with God. In looking for aids to help us pray, we ought to look at the Old and New Testaments as special guides. These guides put both prayer and loneliness into perspective.

If we look at the encounters between man and God that are contained in the Old Testament we can find clues about what can happen between ourselves and God. The stories of Abraham and Moses are classic examples. Volumes have been written about these two figures and other people of the Old Testament. Scripture scholars have analyzed in detail and will continue to analyze the religious meaning that can be learned from studying people of the Old Testament. I am going to single out three aspects of the encounter between the Jewish people of the Old Testament and God, in the hope that consideration of these aspects may help our efforts at prayer.

The first aspect is that the encounter involved a vocation or a call. The encounter was something special, something extraordinary. The encounter had dramatic elements in it. The life of the Jewish people was dramatically changed. God called the Jewish people. In some special way he chose them. This vocation, this call, required a response.

The second element: when the call of God was answered, those who answered were involved in a mission. They had a goal, a task, a function to perform. The Jewish people had a role to play in the history of salvation. Their relations with God were for the purpose of teaching the rest of mankind. Until the end of time, the mission of the people of the Old Testament is to teach the rest of men. The mission of the Jewish people was to prepare for the Savior, to develop themselves religiously, to grow as persons, so that the human race could accept the love explosion that came with Jesus.

The third element that distinguishes the encounter between the Jewish people and God is faith. Both to hear the call of God and to accept the mission given to them, the Jewish people needed faith. The relation between man and God is always surrounded to some extent by darkness. Sometimes the darkness seems extreme. We feel as though God has forgotten about us. At times this was the experience of the Jewish people. In order that the relationship between the people and God be sustained, faith was required. In spite of sufferings and trials, in spite of disappointments and the temptation to disillusionment, faith was needed.

Three Requirements for Prayer
The three characteristics that I have mentioned in relation to the Jewish people of the Old Testa-

ment also apply to our prayer encounter with God.
For prayer to happen, for prayer to be possible,
God must call us. We believe that he has — and
not only that he has but that he *is* calling us. Besides initiating the prayer experience, God's call is
present to us. Prayer is a dialogue. Though, when
we pray, we do not "hear" a divine word or a
divine voice, God is communicating with us. Something is happening to us because of God's presence. The dialogue is genuine. This is difficult to
express because it is difficult to grasp. Yet we believe that a personal God does communicate with
us when we pray.

One aspect of God's communication with us is
that he gives us a mission. Because of God's call
we have a task, a goal, a function. God wants us
to do something. The general lines of what he
wants us to do we know from Sacred Scripture and
revelation. We also have the guides of Church
teaching and exhortation. We know that love
is essential to our mission. We know that in
the dialogue we have with God he is telling us
to be kind, to be concerned about one another,
to be interested in one another's problems.
He is telling us to be concerned about the
poor. We know he wants us to be peacemakers.
He wants us to heal one another. We also know
that he wants us to grow in a knowledge and a love
of his Son. We know God wants us to spread the
good news of Jesus' Resurrection and our share in
his risen life.

However, our entire prayer experience is
wrapped up in faith. While we have heard God's
word through Sacred Scripture, revelation and the
Church's teaching, and while we recognize God's
call and our mission in general categories, we
don't see in detail what we are called to do today
or tomorrow or the next day. All our dealings with
God take place in darkness. Faith is obscure.
While I don't see clearly what God wants me to do

next week, I believe that God is totally involved
in my life. I believe God is intimately interested
in me, not merely in the world but in me. Maybe
this is the most radical act of faith I have to make:
God cares about me. He really does.

This is one of the basic reasons why we need
to pray regularly. I need direct contact with God
so that I can grow, so that I can be tuned in on
the mission I have. I need to encounter God regularly so that I can be sensitive to where he is trying
to lead me and direct me. I need to pray so that
I can stay open to God. If I stay open to God, I will
be open to others.

Often I find prayer difficult. Maybe I shouldn't,
but I do. Yet I hope I don't stop trying to pray.
To stop trying would be like forgetting my roots,
my tradition. It would be like forgetting who I am.
Faith is a light, but it can sometimes seem very
dim. Strange as it seems, it may be at those times
that we can pray best.

The Prayer of Adoration

The prayer which we call adoration involves
man in the most human and most holy type of
encounter. Encounters between people can be
beautiful; they can be personal, deep and freeing.
There is within each person the power to nourish
and help other persons. Human love helps people
be beautiful, helps people to grow spiritually. The
love encounter between people is so mysterious
that we never tire of turning to poets, philosophers,
psychologists, theologians, novelists, dramatists or
anyone we think will be able to deepen our insights.

The encounter between man and God is even
more mysterious. The prayer encounter we call
adoration signifies, better than any other human
activity, what the meaning of man is. At the center
of every prayer experience is God's freedom and

man's freedom. Within these two freedoms are the realities which make adoration the magnificent action it is. Perhaps more than any other human activity, adoration places loneliness in the proper perspective.

None of us can understand how God can create a free person. Throughout Christian history, great thinkers have tried to give people some understanding, some grasp of the interaction between God's free creative act and man's free choices. We can gain some insight into man's freedom, but we can't understand how God can create man and sustain him in freedom. We can't see how God's creative act does not make or force man to act in a definite, prechosen manner.

It helps to remember that God does not create us and then forget about us. He is constantly creating, continually holding us in existence. I cannot write these words without God's constant creative action and you cannot continue to read without God continually giving you your existence. Each part of us is totally created by God. My fingers, my arms, my mind, my ideas — your hands, your eyes, your thoughts — all are dependent on God's continuing creative action. How can God create my freedom? We don't know, but our ignorance should increase — not decrease — our sense of wonder and awe.

The mystery of human freedom is particularly evident when the reality of sin is considered. In creating me, God has created and is creating someone who might reject him for all eternity. Though God wills that I avoid sin, the gift of freedom is so precious that, for the sake of that gift, God allows the danger and risk of sin, the possibility of the creature rejecting the Creator.

To get some understanding of what God does for man when man engages in adoration, a consideration of what happens between two people when they use their freedom in relation to each other may be helpful. Two people can use their freedom toward each other in various ways. They may freely be courteous to each other or freely be abrupt with each other; they may freely love each other or freely hate each other. All these free activities can have important repercussions on each individual's self-image. If some of these free activities take place at a crucial moment they can affect a person's entire life. The free activity which best helps us to understand prayer is the free, loving activity between two people.

Through loving, two people create each other. The self-gift that each person makes to the other serves as a unique power to support and sustain the other in personal living. Each may perform various types of kind actions toward the other and all these actions may spring from love. Perhaps many of these actions are not even noticed by the beneficiary. Think of all that a parent does for a child of which the child is unaware. A person may love so well that the love given becomes part of the atmosphere for the beloved. It becomes like air that the beloved breathes. However, the power, force and beauty of love are particularly evident for most of us when two people face each other and in some symbolic way — a hug, a kiss, a hand-shake, a look — state their love.

Creation Continues

The loving encounter between two persons is something like the prayer encounter. Of the two involved in prayer, one has surrounded the other with love. God's blessings go far beyond man's awareness. Man's most precious gift is his freedom. In prayer he uses that freedom to contact God, to reach the God who has been trying to reach him. In prayer man opens himself to the Love who is creating him and freeing him. This special open-ing of self we call prayer makes a new kind of creation possible. The kind of creation I mean is that through which God's masterpieces, the saints, are created.

I think the most perfect example of what I have been trying to say about prayer is adoration. Man is never more himself than when he adores God. During the time of adoration man puts his life in order; he identifies himself as he turns himself toward God. Adoration is its own reason, its own justification. Man does not adore God for the sake of blessings or favors or requests or to fulfill a law. Man does not adore God so that man will not be lonely even though adoration reveals that man is not alone. Man adores God because God is God and man is man.

The following quotation is from a beautiful essay by Romano Guardini:

> As has been said, we must make a practice of adoration. The important thing is not to wait until obligation requires it, which might happen seldom enough. If we limit ourselves to such occasions, they would grow less and less frequent. . . . At the moment of adoration we are there for God, and for God alone. This very detachment from the oppression of care, from the cravings of the will and from fear is in itself adoration, and floods the soul with truth. Then say: God is here. I am before Him as are those forms in the vision, bowing down before His throne I cannot see, for everything here is still in the obscurity of time, still earthly. But I know by faith that He is here. He is God; I am His creature. He made me; in Him I have my being. . . . And now there is probably no need to write further. The one concerned must look up into the face of God — his God — and tell Him what his heart bids him say.[1]

---

[1]*Faith and Modern Man*, by Romano Guardini, trans. by Charlotte E. Forsyth, © Random House/Knopf.

God freely loves me and freely offers himself in friendship and love to me. God's offer of friendship assures me that I will never be alone again. God offers himself to me. In adoration I say yes.

Chapter Eight

Loneliness and the Christian Life

In this chapter we wish to relate loneliness directly to Christian living, but we want to avoid reducing Christian doctrine to an aspirin or to a guide to mental health. Such reductions destroy the richness of Christianity. Our purpose is to show that living the full Christian life, in addition to all the other benefits that can be attributed to it, is the best way of handling loneliness. Because Christianity speaks to the deepest dimensions of human living, it also speaks to the serious problems of loneliness.

In a secular society in which faith is put under extreme pressure, it is especially important that particular truths about God be stressed. I know of nothing in Christianity more radical and basic than the doctrine of God. We need to remind ourselves over and over that everything in the Christian Church ought to be for man's relationship with God, that every dogma, moral teaching, exercise of authority, pious practice and custom, ought to lead to or deepen the love affair between God and man. If there is any aspect of the Church's life that cannot in some way be linked to the Church's teaching about God, then I don't see why that aspect should be allowed to exist. The Church exists so that man can encounter God. Whatever is an obstacle to man's meeting God should be removed from the Church's life.

For me the primal truth that can keep us enthused about Christianity and willing to struggle through feelings of loneliness that beset us is that God cares about us and has involved himself with us. Though basic to the Christian religion, this truth is difficult to accept. God cares about me. . . . I wonder why and how. At times I feel like questioning whether he does. I feel overwhelmed when I believe he does. The God who created the universe, the God who keeps stars and planets and constellations in existence, is deeply in love with me. This is almost incredible to me. I can't imagine how anyone could prove it. I know that I accept it and I think that acceptance is the only way the truth can be attained. I also know that when I accept it all of reality seems different to me. I'm not alone.

I suppose one reason we find it difficult to believe that God loves us is that we find it so difficult to love one another. Human friendships are tenuous and human love relationships are often short-lived. People easily hurt one another. "Getting even" or "paying back" seems to be a basic human reaction to being hurt. Why does God love us? Why does God continue to involve himself with man? The answers to those questions reveal the meaning of life. The answers are also the heart and soul of Christianity.

Divine-Human Dialogue
No religion emphasizes the value and dignity of a person as much as Christianity. Human life can be looked upon as a dialogue between God and human persons. As in any real dialogue, we must

both listen and respond. First we must listen. This is not always easy. Far from being a passive activity, listening is very active. To listen, we must be genuinely open to the person who is speaking and to what is being said. Sometimes listening demands a deep personal presence. A good model for listening is the therapist or psychological counselor. Some patients who begin therapy think that the counselor should speak more. They complain, "The counselor doesn't do anything, only listens." Never say *only* listens. To listen is an art. By listening well, the counselor may already have begun to help the patient.

In any dialogue the word spoken can at times heal us, at times encourage us, at times challenge us, at times help us know ourselves better. Any dialogue holds out new possibilities for the future; the dialogue with God holds out infinite possibilities.

Rather than being alone, we are people who have been addressed, people to whom a word has been spoken. This word tells us who we are and who God is. The word comforts and consoles us, but also challenges and extols us. In the scenes described in the New Testament, Jesus told his followers a great deal, but now risen and present in his Church, he is still the word being spoken to us by the Father. Jesus has told us and is telling us that God is our Father, that we are of great value to him.

One of the first catechism answers diligently learned by those of us who experienced the question-and-answer catechetical method was "God is everywhere." Wherever being is, infinite Love is creatively present. Sun and moon and stars, trees and rivers and hills, chairs and desks and tables cannot *be* unless God is creatively present to them. The popular song, "He's Got the Whole World in His Hands," expressed imaginatively the truth that all existing reality is due to God's free creative act. God, a spirit who does not have parts, is constantly creating reality from nothing.

Personal Friendship

Most important for our attempts to live the Christian mystery is some understanding of God's special presence to people. Though God is lovingly present to all of creation, the only creature in our experience who can consciously and freely return love is a person. God's presence to a person is different than his presence to the rest of earthly creation. Man is the bodily creature who best can mirror God's intelligent and loving presence. Not only has God created man but we, as Christians, believe that God has invited man into personal relationship, into friendship with himself.

The notion of God's special presence to man is an important truth in the faith of the Jewish people as expressed in the Old Testament. In the mythological account of Adam and Eve, the presence of God is expressed in human terms, but beautifully, by the depiction of God walking in the garden (Gn 3:8). The story of Adam and Eve emphasizes the chief horror of sin: that it makes man distant from God. From Abraham to the Maccabees the identity of the Jewish people is strengthened and supported by their gradually increasing awareness of God's presence among them, the meaning of that presence, the demands of that presence and the beneficial effects of that presence.

A simple comparison may be illuminating. The Jewish people of the Old Testament were like an adolescent growing in self-awareness and maturity. The process of growth is slow, often painful. Self-identity and maturity cannot be achieved without the love and support of others. For the Jewish people's identity, God was the necessary Other. They were a people because of their relation to him. The living presence of God formed

LONELINESS AND THE CHRISTIAN LIFE

them and creatively called them to be his people. Christians believe that the central theme of Old Testament salvation history, the theme of God's loving presence to his people, reaches its perfect expression in the death and resurrection of Jesus.

If we look at the Gospel narratives, we see Jesus going about trying to establish what philosopher Martin Buber calls I-Thou relationships with people. In his public ministry Jesus was the man-for-others, the completely open, creatively present man, telling people they were not alone in an unfriendly universe. Jesus was present, freely offering himself in friendship and inviting people into relationship with his Father. When an individual accepted Jesus' offer, that individual's life was totally transformed. In the man Jesus, people discovered someone to whom they were ready to pledge themselves. The Apostles are obvious examples. Jesus' creative living presence called forth the best in those who accepted him. For Jesus the Apostles left their isolation. God's Word freed them from their loneliness.

Jesus, who on Calvary said a definitive yes to his Father and made possible the salvation of the human race, is telling us that the Father is still calling us. The Father in and through Jesus is offering his love to us. He will, however, not compel us to accept his love. We can freely say yes or no. Yes leads to salvation; no to eternal loneliness. It is our yes to our Father that is the strongest way to combat loneliness. Through that yes we affirm and accept God's love, but we also affirm and accept ourselves as creatures and children of God. Through that yes we say implicitly that we will never be alone again but that we will be people interested in doing our Father's work and in helping our brothers and sisters.

Saying Yes Sacramentally

The presence of God in our lives causes us to

reinterpret all feelings of loneliness. The beautiful
statements of Jesus as reported in St. John's
account of the Last Supper suggest that Jesus was
particularly sensitive to the Apostles' possible sense
of abandonment and loneliness when they could
no longer see Jesus. Today he is sensitive to our
experiences of abandonment and loneliness.
Through all the sacraments, but especially the Eucharist, Jesus comes in a special way to his friends.
As he did 2,000 years ago, he instructs, heals and
calls to courage. The sacraments intensify the relation between the believer and the Father. Saying
yes to the Father is never final or finished but renewed through every growth in love. When a
Christian celebrates a sacrament, especially the
Eucharist, which essentially is Jesus saying yes
through the Christian community, the individual
Christian unites himself or herself more closely to
the Father. With the recent liturgical renewal the
Church has emphasized that the sacraments are
community actions. This entire emphasis stresses
that we are not alone.

Each sacrament could be looked at in relation
to loneliness. If we avoid the danger of reducing
the sacraments to merely emotional tonics or psychological crutches we can see that they have
particular power to help us live through our loneliness. Through Baptism a person is united to a
vibrant, dynamic community of love. The person
dies to self and rises to Christ. At the moment of
Baptism the individual is invited to become a person devoted to others, dedicated to helping others.
This direction is intensified through Confirmation
when the Holy Spirit urges the Christian to spread
the Good News of the kingdom of God, the kingdom of Jesus' followers. Both Matrimony and Holy
Orders are obviously social sacraments. Martin
Buber once described marriage as "taking the other
seriously." The sacramental union between two
persons is supposed to be so intense, so vital, so

loving that they will be a sign to other believers of
the love of Christ for his Church. Holy Orders
calls a person to special service for the community.
It calls a person to be, like Jesus, a man for others.
Both Penance and Anointing of the Sick are healing
sacraments, and without reducing them to merely
emotional supports, it can be said that their power
to help people confront their loneliness is tremendous.

The renewed forms of both sacraments have
special application to loneliness. Penance calls a
person to confront the cause of sin in the roots of
the personality; the sacrament of the Sick, no longer
restricted to those near death, has special power
to heal and to instill courage as the person experiences the horrible loneliness connected with
sickness.

Every aspect of the Eucharist confronts loneliness in a creative way; every aspect of the Eucharist tells us we are not alone. The Eucharist is a
community action. All the members of the community are involved in it. Primarily it is the risen
Jesus' action. He worships the Father through the
members of his Church. Through action and word,
through song and petition, through sign and
symbol, the members of the community worship
their Father and intensify their union with one
another.

In addition to being united to all believers
throughout the world, the Christian is united to deceased members of the Communion of Saints.
When someone we love dies, we tend to think of
him or her as no longer related to us. The deceased
person has achieved his or her reward, while we
must continue to struggle. Yet it seems sensible to
conceive of the deceased as still involved in the
struggle, though in a manner free from pain and
suffering. Having spent a lifetime loving God and
loving God's children, the deceased is more in-

tensely involved in the love life of God after death.
One of the marvelous meanings of the Assumption
is that the Blessed Virgin Mary is involved in the
Christian apostolate. It seems likely that all who
have died in Christ by loving us are encouraging us
in our efforts to help people. This would mean
that my father and sister who are deceased are even
closer to me now than they were when I
could contact them through the senses. They loved
me before they passed through death; they must
love me and be concerned about me at least as
much as they did before they were more intimately joined to the risen Lord. To conceive of the
deceased in this way makes very clear that life is
an adventure in loving and that the adventure does
not stop but quickens after death. The Christian
is involved in a love community where membership
extends beyond the grave. St. Paul in describing
his apostolate wrote: "For I am certain of this:
neither death nor life, no angel, no prince, nothing
that exists, nothing still to come, not any power,
or height or depth, nor any created thing, can
ever come between us and the love of God made
visible in Christ Jesus our Lord" (Rm 8:38, 39).
That's a good description of all of life, both before
and beyond the grave.

Graced Call to Union

The Church's doctrine on the life of grace is
both consoling and challenging to those who are
plagued with loneliness. Limited creatures that we
are, we are called to intimate union with the
Father, Son and Spirit. The eternal love community of the Trinity has chosen to involve us in
their most intimate life. A human person's capacity
for love and knowledge has been widened and
deepened so that he or she can be open to the
Triune God. Perhaps the greatest mystery connected with grace is why God should bother. The
only answer we can come up with is the mystery

of God's love. For some divinely crazy reason God loves us; Father, Son and Spirit have chosen to become involved with us. We share in the love life of the Trinity.

What have traditionally been called the three theological virtues — faith, hope and charity — also call us into relation with God in a special way. To believe in God is to risk one's existence on God. Though faith can be a tremendous comfort, it seems wrong to think of it as making life easy. Faith means much more than merely reciting formulas and creeds. It means committing yourself to a God who may ask anything of you. Love can be terribly demanding. But love is the heart and soul of personal existence. Loneliness can be finally healed only through the God who is love.

Because faith is a risk, hope is required. Believing that God is a Father, the Christian has the courage to hope. At difficult moments in life all can seem dark, but hope can see what eyes cannot see. Christian hope says, "In spite of everything. . . ." There is no way that the Christian can prove to a nonbeliever that hoping in God is the center of personal living. The only "proof" the Christian can offer is his own personal existence: he offers his life as a witness. Like Abraham hoping against hope, the Christian gives the Father of Jesus infinite credit.

The Christian life can be looked at as a love life. From the moment of Baptism to the moment of death, the virtue of charity should be more and more operative in the Christian's life. Opened to Father, Son and Holy Spirit at Baptism, the loving friendship between the believer and God should be a dynamic growing relationship. As he or she loves God more intensely, the Christian's love of others should also deepen and grow. The Christian life calls a person out to others. It is a life of dying to self and giving to others. As the Christian becomes more present to the God who is always lovingly present, so he or she becomes more present to others.

How a Christian's loving presence, his charity in action, will be translated in specific situations will vary greatly, depending on what vocation an individual chooses. Some may do it as fathers or mothers of families; some through the single life; some through the priesthood or religious life. The forms of life are many, but the driving force behind them is one: love. It is love that should dictate the choice of vocation and the choice of life-style. No one person can do everything to help all people, but every person can do something to help some people.

Choosing the Christian life is the best way to handle loneliness. The Christian mystery reveals to us why we feel lonely. We feel alone not because we are alone or abandoned or lost but because there is within us a tremendous need to love and be loved — ultimately a tremendous need to love and be loved by God. If a person chooses not to love God and not to accept God's love, then the person wishes to be completely alone, radically frustrated, totally isolated, which is probably as good a description of hell as any. The Christian mystery expressed in the life, death and resurrection of Jesus reveals how to handle loneliness. To love others is the best and most direct way to handle your feelings of loneliness. The Christian mystery reveals that by dying we live, by giving ourselves away we increase, by being unselfish we become better selves.

Conclusion

Our meditation on loneliness is coming to an end. Can we weave together the various strands of insight into a practical pattern of living so that we can deal with loneliness creatively? Of course, each person who agrees with the basic thrust of this book will put it all together in his or her own way, but perhaps some summary suggestions can be made.

Crucial to dealing with loneliness is understanding it, realizing that it will play some role in each person's life until that person passes through death. The most practical step toward dealing with loneliness can seem to be the least practical step: understand loneliness as deeply and thoroughly as you can. Reflection on the meaning of loneliness is not abstract or speculative in the sense of being impractical. Understanding something is the first step toward handling it. The importance of understanding loneliness can't be overemphasized. To understand loneliness is to begin to win the battle against it. Try to see loneliness as part of the human condition. For the most profound understanding of loneliness, appeal must be made to the meaning of Christianity. Each chapter in this book is a piece of a mosaic which portrays loneliness in different colors and ultimately in the widest possible perspective. Loneliness can be used to reveal the meaning of personal existence and that is what this book has attempted to do.

If someone is convinced of the basic themes of this book but is looking for suggestions to put them into practice, I would suggest that special attention be paid to three areas of human living. The first area is friendship. For most people friendship is the clue to handling loneliness. A person without friends is going to have an extremely difficult time keeping loneliness in place. In battling loneliness the key is to come out of yourself, to open yourself to others. Loneliness tends to enclose us. Friendship opens us. For the person who has come to understand loneliness but now wants to do something about his or her loneliness, I suggest a gradual growing and deepening of relationship with one or two friends. Most people have friends but the lonely person may find it difficult to be open and sharing. To some extent everyone finds this difficult. But by gradually trying to share more deeply, the lonely person will die to loneliness and rise to loving. This kind of effort will affect all the lonely person's relationships and feelings, even religious feelings. In moving out toward friends the person may find that he or she is also moving toward God. In developing and deepening friendships the person should be concerned about giving rather than getting, helping rather than being helped. Of course, the paradox of human existence is that the giver often gains more than he gives.

The second area of human activity centers on patterns of activity. If a person finds loneliness becoming a serious problem, examination and analysis of patterns of activity can be very helpful. Each person has his or her own life-style and some life-styles may be hampering rather than helping the person. Rather than aiding personal growth a life-style may be turning the person inward in an unhealthy way. Are you alone too much? Do you have any hobbies or consuming interests? Does your job help or hinder your battle with loneliness? Does your recreation help you to be less lonely? After looking over the patterns of activity in his or her life, perhaps with a friend or some type of counselor or advisor, a person by a few changes in those patterns of activity can dramatically change the mood surrounding his or her life. A weekly bowling date, a weekly trip to the movies, a weekly discussion group or weekly visits to the sick or aged can redirect a person's energies and interests and put loneliness in a different perspective.

The third area of human living is feelings. Our feelings tell us about ourselves. They send us messages. There are no unimportant feelings. Each has a message for us. For most of us a lifetime is not long enough to read all the messages correctly, but we can gain some insight into them and through them into ourselves. What makes me feel lonely? When does it happen? What do I do that makes it happen? What have I found that helps? By being in touch with my feelings I can deal with loneliness creatively. If I am in touch with my feelings loneliness does not do something to me, but I do something with it. I can use it for personal growth.

One last suggestion I offer is that our basic approach to loneliness should be marked by trust and confidence. I know charity is the most important virtue and that it is the center of the Christian life, but trust must be right behind it. If what has been said in this book about loneliness is true, if our Father has sent his Word to show us how to live, then we ought to be confident that we will be able to handle loneliness with God's help and the resources he has placed within us and at our disposal. Indeed, we can even grow through the experience of it.

Loneliness can be frightening. It needn't be. To be human is to be lonely. Loneliness, when it is properly understood, can be looked on as a gift from God. Loneliness can be an opportunity for insight and growth. Loneliness can be viewed as a call deep within our being, a call telling us who we are and telling us what we should do. Like every other aspect of human nature, loneliness has a purpose. Loneliness is for loving.